Praise for
GROWING FEEL

Growing Feelings translates top-notch psychological science into a clear and compassionate guide that will help kids understand their emotions and the role they play in building and maintaining friendships. This warm, wise, accessible book belongs in the hands of every elementary-school aged child.

Lisa Damour, PhD, author of *Untangled, Under Pressure,*
and *The Emotional Lives of Teenagers*

A great follow-up to *Growing Friendships*! The thinking and research behind this book are sophisticated, but the concepts and strategies are presented in a way that's accessible and empowering for children. Reading this groundbreaking book aloud with your child is a great way to help them gain essential tools for navigating feelings about friends.

Amy McCready, founder of Positive Parenting Solutions
and author of *The "Me, Me, Me" Epidemic*

At a time when so many kids are overwhelmed by understanding their feelings, this charming book provides the perfect combination of humor, strategies, and practical explanations. The authors systematically tackle three big buckets of feelings (anxiety, anger, and sadness) and how they relate to making and keeping friends. Chapters provide relevant examples of real-life experiences and questions through the lens of kids' perspectives. An essential tool for parents, therapists, and educators and an informative and fun guide for students!

Michelle Garcia Winner, founder of Social Thinking

Funny and relatable, *Growing Feelings* takes the sting out of friendship problems. Young readers will emerge feeling better about themselves, with skills to handle jealousy, disappointment, shyness, anger, and more.

Dawn Huebner, PhD, author of *Dr. Dawn's Mini Books about Mighty Fears*

I wish I'd had *Growing Feelings* when I was a kid. This thoughtful and insightful book will help children understand and gracefully navigate the many feelings that come with growing friendships.

Melinda Wenner Moyer, author of *How to Raise Kids Who Aren't Assholes*

Growing Feelings is a fun, engaging discovery guide to the art of growing up. It doesn't simply tell kids about the unique feelings and emotions they have in friendships while growing up but teaches them the story of those feelings and emotions so kids can better enjoy the story they are living.

Matthew Murrie, creator of Curiosity-Based Thinking
and coauthor of *The Book of What If...?*

Managing and coping with our emotions about friends can be tough, especially for kids. With *Growing Feelings*, kids can delve into each Feelings Story and develop a stronger understanding behind the *what*, *why*, and *how* when it comes to the emotions they're experiencing.

Elisa Medhus, MD, founder of Channeling Erik and author of
My Son and the Afterlife and *Raising Children Who think for Themselves*

A fun, engaging, and helpful book for kids to read with their parents! Friendships are critical to healthy development and create many BIG feelings. Dr. Kennedy-Moore and Christine McLaughlin help kids navigate Friendship Rough Spots by helping them understand the multiple emotions they're experiencing and providing a variety of practical actions they can take to improve friendships.

Mary K. Alvord, PhD, psychologist and coauthor of *The Action
Mindset Workbook for Teens, Conquer Negative Thinking for Teens,*
and *Resilience Builder Program for Children and Adolescents*

Children must read this book! It's great—reader-friendly, informative, relevant, and research-based. With its helpful tips, glossary, and fine-tuned perspectives on feelings, actions, reactions, and friendship-building, *Growing Feelings* is destined to become a classic!

Dr. Joanne Foster, gifted education and child development specialist and
award-winning author of *Being Smart about Gifted Education* and *Bust Your BUTS*

Growing Feelings is the kind of book you want to keep close on your desk as a parent or teacher and have additional copies for your kids to keep close for their own reference! In vivid language, with compelling and fun visuals, this book helps readers understand that our feelings aren't here to shame us or make us think there's something wrong with us. Instead, our feelings teach us, help us grow, and through being honest about them, we can become healthier and more hopeful. I love and appreciate this book so much!

Luke Reynolds, PhD, professor of education, Endicott College
and author of *Surviving Middle School, Fantastic Failures,*
and *Braver than I Thought*

A KIDS' GUIDE TO
Dealing with Emotions
about Friends and Other Kids

GROWING FEELINGS

Dr. Eileen Kennedy-Moore
& Christine McLaughlin

BEYOND WORDS
Portland, Oregon

BEYOND WORDS

1750 S.W. Skyline Blvd., Suite 20
Portland, OR 97221-2543
503-531-8700 / 503-531-8773 fax
www.beyondword.com

This Beyond Words paperback edition July 2023

The vignettes in this book are based on composites of children we have known. Names and identifying information have been changed or omitted. The dialogues are fictional. They are intended to represent typical behavior and problems, and they do not refer to specific people or real events.

This book is for general educational purposes only. It does not constitute and should not substitute for individual professional advice, psychotherapy, or the provision of psychological services.

BEYOND WORDS PUBLISHING and colophon are registered trademarks of Beyond Words Publishing. Beyond Words is an imprint of Simon & Schuster, Inc.

For more information about special discounts for bulk purchases, please contact Beyond Words Special Sales at 503-531-8700 or specialsales@beyondword.com.

Managing Editor: Lindsay S. Easterbrooks-Brown
Copyeditor: Ali Shaw, Indigo: Editing, Design, and More
Proofreader: Ashley Van Winkle
Design: Sara E. Blum
The text of this book was set in Adobe Garamond Pro.

Manufactured in the United States of America

10 9 8 7 6 5 4 3 2 1

Library of Congress Cataloging-in-Publication Data

Names: Kennedy-Moore, Eileen, author. | McLaughlin, Christine, author.
Title: Growing feelings : a kids' guide to dealing with emotions about friends
    and other kids / Dr. Eileen Kennedy-Moore and Christine McLaughlin.
Description: Portland, OR : Beyond Words, 2023. | Audience: Ages 6-10
Identifiers: LCCN 2023006140 (print) | LCCN 2023006141 (ebook) |
    ISBN 9781582708782 (paperback) | ISBN 9781582708799 (ebook)
Subjects: LCSH: Friendship in children--Juvenile literature. | Emotions in
    children—Juvenile literature.
Classification: LCC BF723.F68 K453 2023 (print) | LCC BF723.F68 (ebook) |
    DDC 155.4/124—dc23/eng/20230413
LC record available at https://lccn.loc.gov/2023006140
LC ebook record available at https://lccn.loc.gov/2023006141

To my sister, Sheila Kennedy Hickey,
and my brother, Ken Kennedy,
because you're great friends I can always
count on for fun, laughter, and comfort!
EKM

To my dear parents, Marge and Joe Matturro,
for all your love, laughs, and support throughout my life.
CM

CONTENTS

NOTE TO GROWN-UPS

How children handle their feelings about friends can have a big effect on whether their friendships continue, grow stronger, fade, or fall apart.

Research shows that children who know how to manage their emotions are more empathetic, better liked by their peers, less likely to be bullied, more available for learning, better at coping with stress, and generally happier.

Unfortunately, the typical advice that kids get about how to handle feelings is often not helpful. One-size-fits-all recommendations along the lines of "Don't worry" or "Take deep breaths" can leave kids feeling frustrated and lost. "Just calm down" advice isn't easy to follow when kids are upset with a friend, and it also doesn't explain what kids should say or do to maintain or improve their friendships. Also, some of the advice that kids routinely hear, such as suggestions that they punch a pillow when they're mad, is just plain wrong. A mountain of empirical evidence says that acting aggressively rehearses and intensifies anger.

Growing Feelings empowers your child to have a much deeper and more nuanced perspective on feelings about friends. This book helps kids understand themselves and others so they can communicate effectively and build meaningful friendships, and ultimately have more joy in their lives. It also explains the useful functions of all emotions, including painful ones.

Some kids will want to read this book on their own, but we recommend reading it with your child so you can connect the ideas to your child's real-life experiences. There's a lot of information here, so take your time reading it. Whether you start at the beginning or jump to the sections that are most relevant for your child right now, you'll find real help and lots to think and talk about within these pages.

INTRODUCTION FOR KIDS: WHY A BOOK ABOUT FEELINGS AND FRIENDS?

Everyone likes the ideas of "best friends forever" and "happily ever after." But friendships are not that simple. Making and keeping friends can often involve dealing with complicated feelings.

Most kids care a lot about having good friends. So when you hit a **Friendship Rough Spot**, which is when friends disagree, upset, or annoy each other, you're likely to have big feelings in response.

* Maybe you can think of a time when you felt angry or hurt about something a friend said or did.

* Maybe you've felt anxious or guilty, worrying about how a friend reacted to something you did.

* Maybe you've felt sad about being left out or jealous when a friend spent time with someone else.

All of these feelings are very common. How you handle these feelings can have a big effect on whether your friendships last.

This book can help you understand and cope with feelings in ways that build strong and happy friendships. **Happy** friendships mean you care

> Feelings are our inner responses to what's happening in and around us.

about each other, and you feel good when you're together. Even happy friendships sometimes have disagreements and misunderstandings, but you can figure out ways to get past those rough spots.

We're going to look at lots of different feelings about friends and lots of ways to deal with them. But first, let's talk a little bit about what feelings are and how they work.

SOME FACTS ABOUT FEELINGS

Feelings are our inner responses to what's happening in and around us. *Emotions* are specific feelings, such as anger, fear, sadness, jealousy, or happiness.

Feelings are kind of like smells: they can be pleasant or unpleasant, mild or intense, and they give us information we need so we can know what's going on and what it might mean to us.

Wait! Feelings are like smells? Now I'm really interested! I love smells! You know what would be great? A cologne that smells like dog breath! That would be amazing! I'd wear it every day!

Uh. I think you've got that covered . . . without the cologne.

Here are a few important facts about feelings:

* You can have more than one feeling at the same time. That's very common.

* Feelings can change. Whatever you're feeling now, in two hours or two days or two weeks, you'll probably be feeling something different.

* What you think and do have a big effect on how you feel and on how strong your friendships are.

We're going to draw on all of these facts to help you understand the big feelings that come up about friends and other kids. We'll look at ways to think about feeling-filled situations that can help you deal with painful emotions. We'll also talk about when and how to communicate your feelings so that you and your friends can get along better and become closer.

Huh. It's true that some of my biggest feelings have been about things that have happened with friends: I've felt excited and happy, but I've also felt anxious and disappointed and mad and . . .

That sounds unnecessarily complicated. Cats only have two feelings: annoyed and content. Mostly annoyed.

To deal with feelings, we need to understand how they work.

Here's a picture of a *Feelings Story*. It describes how what we think, feel, and do all influence each other. Let's take a look at each of the ingredients of a Feelings Story.

FEELINGS STORY INGREDIENTS

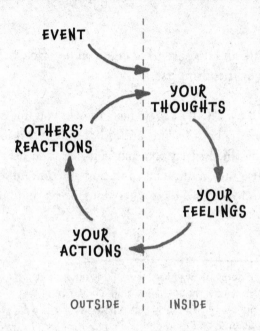

A Feelings Story begins with an ***event***—something happens involving you and a friend. Then you immediately have ***thoughts***, which are your ideas about what that event or situation means for you. Your thoughts then trigger feelings, and your feelings can lead you to take certain ***actions***, which means doing something. Your actions can lead to other people's ***reactions***, which are what they think or do in response to what you did. Their reactions can be like a new event that gets the whole circle of a Feelings Story going around again.

Thoughts and feelings are invisible because they happen inside us, but our actions and others' reactions happen where people could see them.

Understanding Feelings Stories is easier if we look at a specific example. Let's imagine Yusef strikes out Finn in kickball. That single event can have very different meanings, which can lead to very different feelings and even different relationships.

TWO VERSIONS OF A FEELINGS STORY: FINN'S RESPONSE TO BEING STRUCK OUT BY YUSEF

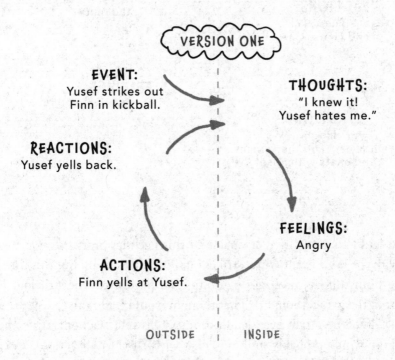

VERSION ONE

EVENT:
Yusef strikes out
Finn in kickball.

THOUGHTS:
"I knew it!
Yusef hates me."

REACTIONS:
Yusef yells back.

FEELINGS:
Angry

ACTIONS:
Finn yells at Yusef.

OUTSIDE | INSIDE

In version one of this Feelings Story, Finn thinks Yusef doesn't like him, so he probably expects and notices mean actions from Yusef. When Yusef strikes him out in kickball, Finn might think, "I knew it! He hates me!" (thought). This belief—that the strike is proof that Yusef hates him— would make Finn feel angry (feeling) and could lead him to yell at Yusef (action). Then Yusef might yell back (reaction), and Finn would be even more convinced that Yusef hates him. Meanwhile, Yusef probably wasn't thinking much about Finn until Finn started yelling at him.

VERSION TWO

EVENT:
Yusef strikes out
Finn in kickball.

THOUGHTS:
"Yusef likes me."
"This is just part of
the game."

REACTIONS:
Yusef smiles back
and chats.

FEELINGS:
Calm

ACTIONS:
Finn laughs, says,
"Oh, well!" and then smiles
and chats with Yusef.

OUTSIDE | INSIDE

Now, let's look at a different version of this Feelings Story. Version two starts with the same event: Yusef strikes out Finn in kickball. But this time, suppose Finn thinks Yusef *does* like him, and he realizes the strikeout is just part of the game (thought). That thought would lead Finn to feel *calm* (feeling). Then he might even laugh or say, "Oh well!" (action). After the game, Finn would probably smile and chat with Yusef (more action). Yusef would likely smile and chat back (reaction), so Finn would be even more convinced that Yusef is a nice guy.

These examples show that *our feelings don't happen directly because of an event.* There's a step between the event and our feelings: our thoughts about the event lead to our feelings. Also, our thoughts and feelings can lead us to act in ways that create new events that make the Feelings Story keep going around.

The good news is that each step in a Feelings Story is something we can work on if we want to change how we feel and build meaningful friendships.

This book talks about lots of different feelings about friends. For clarity, we've separated them into *Feelings Families*, which are groups of similar feelings, but it's common to have more than one feeling at the same time, from the same or a different feeling family.

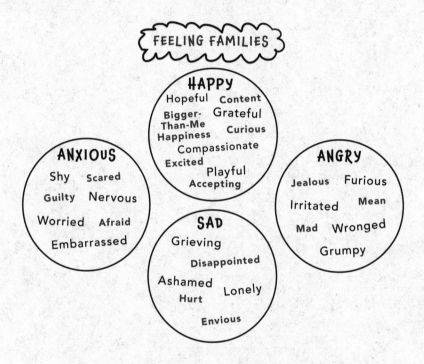

Let's start by looking at feeling anxious about friends.

PART I
Feeling Anxious about Friends

Feeling *anxious* involves worrying about something bad happening. When we're feeling anxious about friends, it usually means we're worried that other kids won't like us.

Anxiety is uncomfortable, but it can be useful. It makes us aware of what others want or expect from us. Caring about other people's feelings helps us to be a good friend. People who don't care at all about what anyone else thinks tend to act like jerks. Anxiety can also give us energy to try to be friendly. But if we're too anxious, it can hold us back from wanting to be around others or letting them get to know us.

Here are some ideas for dealing with feeling anxious about friends.

1

Feeling Shy

LUIS'S CHALLENGE: NERVOUS ABOUT GOING TO A PARTY

Feeling *shy* means being uncomfortable around people you don't know well because you're not sure what to say or do, and you're worried they won't like you. When people feel shy, they are *nervous*—or anxious and jumpy inside—about social situations and will often try to avoid them.

Luis is afraid to go to the party because he doesn't know anyone there besides the birthday boy, Justin. He's probably imagining that he'll be standing silently and awkwardly in a corner while everyone else is chatting and having fun. Maybe he also pictures kids staring at him and thinking he's weird. This scares him and makes him want to hide.

Part of the problem is that Luis is viewing Justin's birthday party as a place where he must perform, as if he were on stage. He imagines all the other kids judging him, and he thinks he has to say clever things to impress everyone.

Do you think Justin expects Luis to amaze everyone at the party? Probably not. He just likes Luis and wants to spend time with him. If Luis doesn't go to the party, it could hurt Justin's feelings. To **hurt** someone means to do something that causes pain. Hitting or kicking could hurt someone's body, but it's also possible to hurt someone's feelings by doing something that leads them to feel sad or upset. If Luis doesn't come to the party, Justin might think Luis doesn't care about him.

Skipping Justin's party also means Luis would be letting his anxious feelings cause him to miss out on having fun and maybe making new friends.

FEELINGS STORY: LUIS'S RESPONSE TO BEING INVITED TO JUSTIN'S BIRTHDAY PARTY

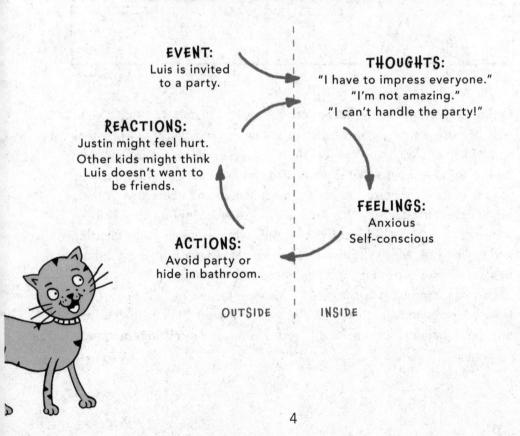

EVENT:
Luis is invited to a party.

THOUGHTS:
"I have to impress everyone."
"I'm not amazing."
"I can't handle the party!"

REACTIONS:
Justin might feel hurt. Other kids might think Luis doesn't want to be friends.

FEELINGS:
Anxious
Self-conscious

ACTIONS:
Avoid party or hide in bathroom.

OUTSIDE | INSIDE

4

The event that sets Luis's Feelings Story in motion is the party invitation. He responds to this event by thinking that he has to be extremely clever or funny or cool so that the other partygoers in the "audience" will like him. But he doesn't believe he's extremely clever or funny or cool, so he thinks that he can't handle the party. This makes him feel anxious and awkward, so he decides he has two options: avoid the party completely or hide in the bathroom (actions).

What reactions are those actions likely to get from other kids? Justin's feelings might be hurt, and the other partygoers will think Luis doesn't want to be friends with them, so they'll be less friendly to him. His Feelings Story is actually creating the situation he's scared of, which is people not liking him!

Luis is putting way too much pressure on himself! He doesn't have to impress anyone; he just needs to find ways to be part of the fun. This is easier than he thinks.

Find ways to be part of the fun.

Here are some possibilities that you might want to try if you feel nervous about a party or other gathering.

BE A SOCIAL DETECTIVE

You can be a *Social Detective* by watching carefully to figure out what other kids are doing in a certain situation. That's a big clue for what *you* could be doing too.

For example, in Luis's case, when he arrives at the birthday party, the first thing he could do is look around to see where other kids have put their presents and put his present there too. Next, if the weather is cool, he could look around to see where other kids have put their coats and put his coat there. Then he could look for the birthday boy and say hi to him. Finally, he could look to see what the other kids are doing and do the same thing. For instance, if other kids at the party are lining up to hit a piñata, he should line up for his turn too.

Noticing what other kids are doing can help you figure out what to do if you're not sure how to join the fun.

Obviously, if you see some kids doing things that could hurt or upset someone or break something, you shouldn't do what they're doing. Look around to find better examples. If it's a serious problem, you could quietly and privately tell an adult. If it's not that serious, ignore it. You're not in charge of making other kids behave well, and tattling is not a good way to make or keep friends.

If you're invited to a big party, you may want to arrive on the early side, so it's less hectic when you first get there. That makes it easier to look around and see what other kids are doing. You might even get a bit of one-on-one time to connect with the kid who invited you, before the action really starts.

SMILE AND NOD

Some kids feel anxious around a bunch of other kids because they don't know what to say. Here's a secret: you don't necessarily have to say anything! You can use your face and body to join in. Just stand near a group, smile to show you like them, nod when it's appropriate, and maybe even laugh along. As you become more comfortable, you may decide to speak up, but you don't have to. Even without saying a word, you're still participating and adding to the fun because you're there! Not everyone has to be a noisy, attention-grabbing star of the party. A quieter style of being friendly is just fine.

TALK TO ONE PERSON AT A TIME

It can feel overwhelming if you think about having to talk to a whole group of people, especially if you don't know them well.

Try concentrating on just one person at a time. This one person could be the kid who happens to be next to you, or you could look around the room for someone who seems friendly but isn't involved in a conversation and go talk to that kid. You don't have to know someone well—or at all—to start a conversation.

But what should you say? Here are some conversation tips you might want to try:

7

Offer a sincere compliment. You might want to start with a compliment, such as "I like your shoes" or "Your hair looks nice like that" or "Wow! Great catch!" But only say a compliment if you really mean it.

Look for common ground. *Common ground* is what is true of both you and someone else. That's where friendships grow. If you're at a party with someone, two things you have in common are the friend who invited you both and being at the party.

Asking questions can help you figure out what else you have in common. Try asking a question that begins with "how" or "what," so you get more than a short, yes/no answer. This helps keep the conversation going.

In Luis's case, he might ask, "How do you know Justin?" or "What's your favorite sport?"

Sometimes you can notice clues that point to common ground. For instance, if a kid is wearing a T-shirt about a movie or a collectible you like, you could say, "Cool T-shirt! I like that too!" then ask a question to understand more about that person's interest in the topic, such as "What do you think about the new movie?" or "What do you think about the new series?"

Be careful not to brag. Also be careful not to put yourself down. Neither is friendly. A fun conversation is about getting to know the other person, letting them get to know you, and figuring out what you have in common. It's not about judging yourself.

Let the activity guide your conversation. It's often easiest to talk with someone when you're doing something together. For example, if you're playing a game, you can talk about the game. If you're eating pizza, you can talk about the pizza.

If you're very involved in an activity with other kids, conversation is likely to flow directly from the activity, without you having to think much about it. You may want to describe what's happening ("The score is 7 to 7.") or ask something that fits with the activity ("Could

8

you please pass the napkins?"). Sometimes, just making a comment will start up a conversation.

Move on, if needed. If the first person you try to talk with doesn't really respond, that's OK. No one ever died from or even got seriously injured by an awkward conversation. Just end the conversation by saying, "Well, I'm going to [fill in the blank: get a drink, play the game, look for the birthday kid]. See you later." Then walk away and try talking with someone else. If you're sitting down or standing in line, so it's not easy to walk away, you can just turn to the person on the other side of you and try talking with that person.

RESPOND POSITIVELY WHEN SOMEONE ASKS YOU A QUESTION

In addition to reaching out to talk to people, you also want to respond in friendly ways if someone asks *you* a question. Often, people ask questions that are some version of "How are you?" or "How's it going?" Whenever possible, a useful way to answer this type of question is by using the *Great-Plus-One-Fact Formula*.

The "great" part expresses enthusiasm. That's important because it makes the conversation more enjoyable. In general, it's polite to be positive rather than negative with people you don't know well.

The "one fact" part should be something that creates a picture in the listener's mind. That makes your answer interesting and helps the conversation flow.

Here's an example:

Wow! That's a good answer! She could have said, "Terrible! We haven't won a game all season!" but that's a downer. It's not pleasant to listen to someone complaining. Instead, this kid found some positive things to talk about—cheering and good snacks—that the listener can easily imagine. And the conversation can continue from there. Don't you want to know what kind of snacks they have?

Now you try answering a question in a friendly way. Here's the question: *How was your weekend?*

What could you say in response? Use the Great-Plus-One-Fact Formula. Start with "Great!" and then describe one thing that you *honestly* think was great and that creates a picture in the listener's mind. Don't lie. Do look for the positive. It was a whole weekend. If you think carefully, you're likely to be able to come up with *something* that was great.

What if you only want to say "Good!" instead of "Great!"? Or what if the thing was only "OK"? Try to aim for "Great!" It's not that you have to feel great all the time—no one does—but somewhere in your life there is something that you honestly feel is great. It's good practice to notice those things. Also, people who express real enthusiasm are fun to be around.

Think about the kids below and their answers to the question, "How was your weekend?" Who would you rather talk with?

If you're like most people, you'd prefer to talk with any of the kids except the first one. The first kid is a weight, dragging down the conversation. The *blah* response sends the message, "I'm not interested in talking with you!" The other kids are bringing up the level of fun in the conversation because they found something to be enthusiastic about. That's a generous thing to do! They're responding kindly to the person trying to talk with them and saying something that can keep the conversation going. Because they're focusing on the positive, they're more fun to talk to. They also probably feel happier.

What if your weekend was really terrible? If you're talking with a close friend, of course you can talk about your problems, but if you don't know the person that well, stick with the Great-Plus-One-Fact Formula. Somewhere in the whole weekend you can probably find something you can be enthusiastic about.

BUILD UP YOUR SOCIAL CONFIDENCE BY DOING BRAVE THINGS

Do you know what it means to be brave? Most kids think being brave means never feeling scared or nervous. But really, being **brave** means doing something *even though* you feel scared.

Feeling anxious is a sign that you're doing something new or challenging, and your brain and body are pumped and ready for action! The more you do things that are *not* dangerous but just *feel* scary, the more confident you'll become that you can handle feeling anxious, and the easier those scary situations will seem.

The reverse is also true: the more you avoid doing things, the scarier they seem. Avoidance makes anxious feelings grow.

In Luis's case, if he decides to skip the party, he might feel relieved at first, thinking, "Phew! I don't have to go to that party!" but the next time he faces a similar situation, it will be even harder to go because he hasn't proven to himself that he can handle it.

If you feel anxious about talking to kids you don't know well, you may want to practice doing exactly that. Little by little, it will become easier. For instance, you could set a goal of saying hi to a certain number of people each day. Or maybe you'd like to try giving someone a sincere compliment or asking someone a question to look for common ground.

Here's what you're likely to find: the worry beforehand is almost always worse than the actual situation. Can you think of a time when you felt very nervous about doing something but then it turned out to be OK or even fun?

If you decide to practice talking with kids you don't know well, you may feel a bit awkward or uncomfortable at first. That makes sense if you haven't done it much. But it probably won't turn out to be the horrible scene you might have imagined. How likely is it that someone will say to you, "What?! How dare you say hi to me!"? Not very likely.

As you stay in the situation, your nervousness is likely to fade as you get used to it. And you might even end up having a good time. The more you put yourself out there with other kids, the easier it will become to do so.

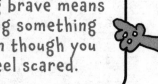

Being brave means doing something even though you feel scared.

2
Feeling Worried

**VIOLET'S CHALLENGE: AFRAID
A FRIEND IS MAD AT HER**

Feeling *fear* means we are experiencing anxiety because we're imagining, "What if something bad happens?"

Violet didn't hear back right away from her friend Shanice, and she's imagining that something is wrong. She is afraid that Shanice is angry with her and no longer wants to be friends. Being *afraid* means feeling anxious about something or someone that you think is likely to hurt or upset you in some way. Getting dumped by Shanice would definitely be upsetting for Violet.

Because she's not sure why Shanice hasn't responded, Violet is worrying about the possibilities. Feeling *worried* means being anxious because we keep thinking about possible problems and how difficult they would be. Worried feelings tend to get bigger as these upsetting thoughts go around and around in our heads. Some kids have a habit of worrying and may

16

spend a lot of time imagining terrible outcomes, which makes them feel even more anxious.

> Just because we can imagine something doesn't make it true.

Violet's built up a whole big and terrible what-if situation in her mind: What if Shanice is mad at her? What if Shanice is deliberately ignoring her? She might even be imagining: What if Shanice doesn't like her anymore? All of this makes Violet feel more and more anxious.

When we don't know something, our imagination can fill in the blanks in ways that make us feel worried. Violet doesn't know why Shanice isn't answering, so she assumes the worst—that Shanice no longer wants to be her friend. But just because we can imagine something doesn't make it true or likely.

Instead of worrying about why Shanice isn't replying, Violet should try howling. Whenever I do that, all the dogs in the neighborhood start howling too. It's like a concert. I bet Shanice would hear that and join right in!

I know I would. Cats are very musical. Let's get this party started right MEOW!

FEELINGS STORY:
VIOLET'S RESPONSE WHEN SHANICE DOESN'T REPLY TO HER MESSAGES

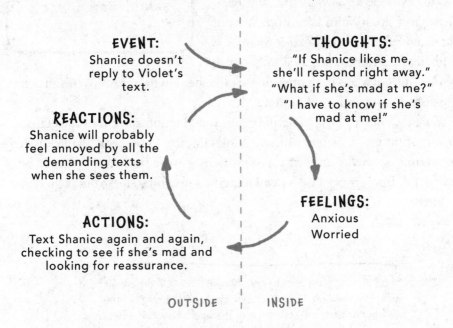

EVENT:
Shanice doesn't reply to Violet's text.

THOUGHTS:
"If Shanice likes me, she'll respond right away."
"What if she's mad at me?"
"I have to know if she's mad at me!"

REACTIONS:
Shanice will probably feel annoyed by all the demanding texts when she sees them.

FEELINGS:
Anxious
Worried

ACTIONS:
Text Shanice again and again, checking to see if she's mad and looking for reassurance.

OUTSIDE | INSIDE

Violet's Feelings Story starts with not getting a response to her message. Her thoughts give meaning to that event. She believes that if Shanice likes her, she'll always respond right away. When that doesn't happen, Violet imagines that Shanice might be mad at her. She also believes she can't stand the uncertainty and has to know right away whether Shanice still likes her. All of these thoughts make Violet feel very anxious and worried, so she starts bugging Shanice with lots of messages. But that's likely to annoy Shanice.

Violet is looking for **reassurance**, which means she wants someone—in this case Shanice—to take away her worries. But all that poking could end up pushing her friend away, which is what she was worried about in the first place.

So what are some useful ways to handle the worries that can come up in a situation like Violet's, when a friend doesn't respond? Here are some ideas.

DON'T MAKE IT A TEST

Try not to view sending a message to a friend as a test of the friendship. It's not fair to your friend to think, "If they respond right away, that means they like me. If they take too long to respond, that means they don't care about me at all!" This puts too much pressure on the friend and attaches too much meaning to small actions.

It's important to have realistic expectations about friends responding. Of course you want a response right away! But with some friends, it could take a day or even a week to get a response. If the message isn't urgent, the friend might not respond at all. That's disappointing, but it might have nothing to do with how the friend feels about you.

THINK OF POSSIBLE REASONS

Violet needs to be careful about jumping to conclusions about *why* Shanice hasn't responded to her messages. If she assumes it's because Shanice doesn't like her, she could be making herself miserable for no reason.

There are lots of reasons why a friend might not respond immediately. Here are some of those reasons. Can you think of more?

* Maybe she's busy doing homework.

* Maybe she got in trouble and her grown-ups took her device away.

* Maybe she's doing something with her family.

* Maybe she doesn't have her device with her because she left it in the other room.

* Maybe she forgot to charge her device.

* Maybe she's sick and not feeling up to chatting.

* Maybe she's tired of being online and is just taking a break.

* Maybe she doesn't like online messaging and is often slow to respond.

* Maybe . . .

Thinking about all the reasons why a friend might not be responding helps you take it less personally. No one is available all the time, so it's not kind or fair to assume that a lack of response means your friend doesn't care about you.

TRUST YOUR FRIENDS TO TELL YOU IF SOMETHING IS WRONG

Sometimes, kids who feel anxious about friends imagine that their friend is rejecting them, even when they're not. If a friend doesn't answer a message or seems a little distracted or talks more to someone else, they jump to the conclusion, "My friend must be mad at me!" They're so afraid of losing friends that they constantly check whether friends are mad at them. Unfortunately, this can create problems.

20

21

Like Violet, the first girl here wants to be reassured that her friend still likes her. But almost as soon as she hears her friend's response, she starts feeling anxious and wondering again, "What if she changed her mind, and *now* she's mad at me?"

And how do all these questions make her friend feel? It may seem like it's a caring thing to ask, "Are you mad at me?" but frequently asking this question is annoying to others. It quickly becomes more about your feelings ("I need you to make my worry go away!") than the other person's feelings.

Part of being a good friend is trusting the other person. Constantly looking for reassurance that someone still likes you is kind of like saying, "I don't trust you!"

Usually when someone is mad at you, it's obvious. Assume your friends will tell you if they're angry. If they don't, assume everything is OK.

GIVE A FRIEND SOME SPACE

For whatever reason, Shanice can't or doesn't want to chat right now. That's OK. Good friends are willing to give each other space when needed. Out of caring for Shanice, Violet needs to leave her alone for now.

Sometimes, when kids are anxious about a friendship, they try too hard, sending a friend lots and lots of messages, one after the other. But this can feel like a one-sided water balloon fight, where one kid is throwing water balloons, and the other kid is just standing there, getting hit. That's no fun for the friend.

Conversations between friends need to be more like a game of catch, where both friends take turns sending and receiving. If you find that you're doing a lot more sending than your friend, you probably need to slow down so it's more even between you two.

Because Shanice isn't responding right now, it would be a good idea for Violet to wait before she sends another message. How long she waits depends on the importance of the message. If, for some practical reason, she needs a response from Violet, she might wait a couple of hours before trying again. She could then send something like, "Hi, sorry to bug you again, but I need to know by tonight if you want my dad to drive you home after the game tomorrow."

If it's not something urgent, she might want to wait a day or two before sending another message. Waiting gives Shanice a chance to reach out to Violet.

Waiting isn't easy, but spending time apart gives friends a chance to miss each other a little bit, so they want to be together. Waiting is an important skill and an unavoidable part of managing anxiety about friends. By waiting, you're training yourself to get used to not knowing for sure. You're not always going to get instant answers, and that's OK. You are strong enough to sit with not knowing why your friend hasn't responded. Trust yourself. Trust your friend.

To feel less bothered by her unresponsive friend, Violet could distract herself by doing something else. She might want to message a different friend, or she might want to put her device down and find a fun activity to do on her own or with someone else. What do you like to do when you have free time?

FOLLOW UP IN A FRIENDLY WAY WHEN A FRIEND HASN'T RESPONDED IN A WHILE

The new message that Violet sends after a day or two should be something friendly. This makes it more likely that Shanice will answer in a friendly way. Violet could:

* Ask about something going on in Shanice's life, such as "How's your new puppy?" or "Have you seen any good movies lately?"

* Share something funny or interesting

* Invite Shanice to do something fun with her

* Express concern for Shanice by sending a message like "Hi, I haven't heard from you in a while. Are you OK?" (Remember those *maybes* you thought of?)

Trust yourself.
Trust your friend.

24

And if Shanice doesn't respond to a second message after a day or two? Violet might want to wait another week and then try messaging again. If Shanice still doesn't reply, Violet will have to conclude that messaging Shanice isn't a good way to connect with her. Maybe that's because they've hit a Friendship Rough Spot or maybe Shanice just doesn't like messaging.

SWITCH TO IN-PERSON COMMUNICATION

If possible, Violet may want to try reconnecting with Shanice in person. Online messages don't show tone of voice, facial expressions, or body language. So, there's a big chance of misunderstanding.

Try this experiment:

1. Say the word "Hello" in an angry tone of voice.

2. Now say "Hello" in a scared tone of voice.

3. Now say "Hello" in an excited tone of voice.

25

What did you notice? These three *hellos* are very different. As you said each of them, your face and body probably changed along with the tone of your voice to show the emotion. But in a message, they all look exactly the same.

This is why it's never a good idea to have an emotional conversation over online messages. Emojis just can't make up for all the emotional meaning that's lost when we communicate with only typed words.

If Violet can see Shanice's body language and talk with her in person, Violet could get a better sense of how their friendship is really going and maybe even put some of her worries to rest.

RECONNECT WITH A FRIEND AFTER A GAP

When they do reconnect, whether it's in person at school the next day or through messaging a while later, Violet definitely shouldn't give Shanice a hard time about her earlier lack of response. Instead, she should just let the past be the past and focus on having a good time together in that moment. Doing fun things together is what builds and strengthens friendships.

Once they've reconnected, Violet could gently ask for what she wants by saying something like, "Could you please try to respond to my messages? I feel anxious (or frustrated, or disappointed) when I send you something and I don't hear anything back." Notice that this statement does several kind things:

* It asks for the specific action Violet wants ("respond to my messages").

* It uses the word "try," so it doesn't demand perfection.

* It uses the word "I" to describe Violet's feelings rather than "you" to criticize Shanice.

But, out of caring for Shanice, Violet may decide not to say anything about the unanswered messages. We don't *have* to comment on everything a friend does or doesn't do that we dislike. Offering extra understanding and forgiveness is good for friendships.

To continue her friendship with Shanice, Violet may have to accept that Shanice is a good friend in many ways but not so good at answering messages.

LET GO OF THE WORK OF WORRYING

Violet is very scared about the possibility of her friendship with Shanice ending. What if Shanice really is mad at her and is deliberately ignoring her?

That's possible. Refusing to talk to someone isn't a smart or kind way to deal with a Friendship Rough Spot, but sometimes it happens. Not every friendship lasts forever.

Violet thinks she has to worry about this bad possibility because it's bad! Worrying takes a lot of effort and energy, so it seems like it's a useful thing to do. But it doesn't prevent bad things from happening. It just makes you unhappy.

Violet could tell herself, "Right here, right now, Shanice hasn't said anything about being mad at me. I'll deal with that when and *if* it happens." That statement focuses on now, which is the moment she's in. It also recognizes that we can't predict the future. And worrying about every bad thing that *might* happen can steal our enjoyment of what's happening now, so it's best not to do that.

If Shanice does end up saying she's mad at Violet, Violet will be in a better position to deal with it after they've spoken, when she knows what's going on, rather than just imagining every bad possibility. Worrying *now* doesn't help Violet be a better friend to Shanice.

Maybe Shanice will reach out later, or maybe she won't. Maybe they'll reconnect once they see each other in person, or maybe they won't. It's hard to accept, but Violet can't make Shanice do anything. What she *can* do is leave the door open to friendship by being ready to respond warmly to Shanice if they connect at a later time.

LOOK FOR MORE FRIENDS

No matter what happens with Shanice, it would be a good idea for Violet to try to reach out to other friends. Who else has she had fun with? Those kids might be open to chatting or getting together.

A larger circle of friends gives more options for fun and puts less pressure on each individual friendship. It's a bit like having more than one favorite shirt. If one is in the laundry or lost somewhere in your room, you can just enjoy the other one, and neither shirt gets worn out.

3

Feeling Embarrassed

JALEEL'S CHALLENGE: SCARED OF BEING THE CENTER OF ATTENTION

The teacher's comments are very positive. She's admiring Jaleel's work, but the experience doesn't feel positive to Jaleel. Instead, Jaleel feels **embarrassed** to be the center of attention. **Embarrassment** means feeling uncomfortably aware of other people noticing you. For Jaleel, this attention feels **scary**, which means it seems dangerous or overwhelming, because he doesn't know how to handle it. He might also worry that his classmates will judge him negatively.

Do you think the teacher wanted Jaleel to feel bad? Definitely not! Most likely the teacher meant to be encouraging by recognizing how well he's doing. But for Jaleel, the attention from the teacher makes him feel very uncomfortable.

30

FEELINGS STORY: JALEEL'S RESPONSE TO PRAISE FROM THE TEACHER

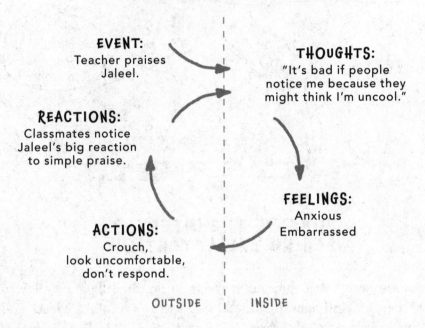

EVENT:
Teacher praises Jaleel.

THOUGHTS:
"It's bad if people notice me because they might think I'm uncool."

REACTIONS:
Classmates notice Jaleel's big reaction to simple praise.

FEELINGS:
Anxious
Embarrassed

ACTIONS:
Crouch, look uncomfortable, don't respond.

OUTSIDE | INSIDE

The event that begins Jaleel's Feelings Story is praise from the teacher. He thinks that it's bad if people notice him because they might think he's dumb or uncool. He then feels anxious and embarrassed about the attention, so he tries to hide from it (action). He slumps awkwardly, looking uncomfortable and saying nothing. But this makes him stand out more, because it makes it obvious that the teacher's simple praise is a big, uncomfortable deal for him. The other kids probably notice this, which makes them stare at him more because they wonder why he's acting that way (reaction). The other kids' reactions confirm Jaleel's thoughts and lead him to feel even more anxious and embarrassed.

Have you ever felt embarrassed by attention, like Jaleel? Here are some ideas about how to deal with that.

THINK OF THE INTENTION BEHIND THE ATTENTION

Intention means what someone is trying to do. By calling attention to what Jaleel is doing right, the teacher hopes to give helpful feedback and encouragement to Jaleel ("Keep doing what you're doing!"). She probably also hopes that Jaleel's classmates will learn from his good example.

Jaleel's embarrassment might ease if he thinks about why the teacher called on him. Despite what we might fear, teachers don't call on kids to "catch" them; they do it to make sure everyone understands what they're trying to teach. If you get the answer right, fine. The teacher will move on. If you get the answer wrong, that's OK because other kids in your class are probably confused too.

> Kids think they're supposed to get everything right, but teachers actually love it when they can help kids.

Here's a secret: Kids think they're supposed to get everything right, but teachers actually love it when they're able to help kids move from not understanding something to understanding it. If you get the answer wrong, your

32

teacher is likely to think, "Yay! I get to *teach* someone! That's the whole reason I'm here! I want to *teach* kids, and now I get to do that!"

KNOW YOUR AUDIENCE

Many kids are scared of being called on in class. The idea that everyone is looking at them and judging them makes them feel awkward and self-conscious. *Self-conscious* means being uncomfortably aware of everything you might be doing wrong or everything about you that's not perfect.

But what are you thinking when you hear someone else get called on in class? You're probably not thinking, "Ah! Now is a chance for me to judge how much my classmates know and decide whether or not they're smart!" If you're like most kids, you'll pay attention if your classmate says something that's useful for you, but mostly you're either not that interested in what your classmate says, or you're thinking, "Thank goodness I wasn't the one called on!" Your classmates are probably thinking the same things when you get called on.

STAY IN THE WATER TO GET USED TO IT

Unfortunately, just telling yourself that the other kids aren't judging you probably isn't enough to get past your discomfort with attention. You're going to have to prove to yourself that attention isn't dangerous.

Getting used to attention is like getting used to the water when you go swimming. Think about what happens right after you jump into a pool. How do you feel? Usually, you think, "Yikes! The water is freezing!" But what happens if you stay in the water? Does the water temperature change? Nope! What changes is your perception of the water. After a while, it doesn't feel so cold anymore because you get used to it.

Some people like to jump right into the water. Others prefer an inch-by-inch approach. Either way is fine. The important thing to remember is that *no amount of standing at the edge of the pool will get you used to the water.*

You Can't Get Used to the Water by Staying out of It

In other words, no amount of avoiding attention is going to help you get used to it. To get over being scared of attention, you could try this: set a goal for yourself to raise your hand to ask or answer a question once every class period.

What?! Why would you do such a thing when you hate attention and feel embarrassed when you get called on?

Can you guess? If you raise your hand, you get some control over when the attention happens, which makes it easier to deal with.

But, more importantly, how do you think you'll feel around the fortieth time you've been called on? Will it be harder or easier than the first few times? It might take a while, but the more you practice speaking in class, the easier it will become. Whether you get the answer right or wrong, whether your question is brilliant or ordinary or basic, it doesn't

> If you keep speaking up, over time, it'll get easier.

matter. If you keep speaking up, over time, it'll get easier, and your embarrassment will ease as you become more comfortable with attention.

You may never like being the center of attention, but you'll prove to yourself that you can handle it.

RESPOND POLITELY TO A COMPLIMENT

In Jaleel's case, the attention the teacher gives him is positive. She's not pointing out a mistake—she's praising Jaleel! But Jaleel feels embarrassed by the unwanted attention in part because he doesn't know how to respond.

This is an easy one to solve: when someone gives you a compliment, just say, "Thank you." That's all. You don't have to explain or put yourself down. Just respond with a simple "Thank you."

Look at the difference between these two responses to a compliment:

Response One

Response Two

How do you think the compliment-giver feels in each version of this scene? In the first version, the arguing response probably made the compliment-giver feel uncomfortable. Maybe even a bit insulted. She was trying to say something kind about her friend's sweater, but in response she got a whole speech about why the sweater isn't nice.

The first compliment-receiver wasn't trying to be mean. Maybe she felt embarrassed by the attention, or maybe she was trying to be modest, but instead she ends up implying that the compliment-giver has bad taste! She also drags out the interaction in a way that's probably not fun for either of them.

In the second version of this scene, the compliment-receiver responds with a quick thanks, and then she moves on. This probably leaves the compliment-giver feeling good.

A compliment is like a small gift. When we give someone a gift, we hope the receiver likes it and says thank you. If she wants, the compliment-receiver could add a return compliment, such as "Yours is pretty too." That would be like giving a gift back. But she doesn't have to. A simple "Thanks" is enough.

Here are two more compliments. How do you think the compliment-receivers should respond to them?

Should the compliment-receiver respond, "Yeah, but I missed a bunch of other shots, and Misha scored more than me"? Definitely not! That would squash the compliment and could make the compliment-giver feel bad. Instead, the compliment-receiver should just say, "Thanks!"

What do you think should happen here? Should the compliment-receiver say, "It's not *that* good. Anyone could have done it. And besides, the back is kind of crooked"? No. It doesn't make sense to argue when you're given a compliment. You know how they should respond: just say, "Thanks!"

HANDLE MISTAKES AROUND OTHER PEOPLE

Sometimes kids feel embarrassed because they make a mistake and every-one looks at them. Maybe you've had experiences where you tripped, or you bumped into someone in a clumsy way, or you dropped something and made a big mess, or you put your sweatshirt on backwards, with the tag sticking out. These errors don't really hurt anyone, but you probably felt embarrassed because they were noticeable to others. Missteps are especially embarrassing when someone we want to impress sees them.

Keep in mind that blunders happen to everyone. Most likely, when you messed up, people came to help or at least sympathized. We've all been there.

So if you goof up in front of other people, just say, "Oops!" or maybe, "Big oops!" That lets you admit the error but also shows it wasn't on purpose. Do what you can to set things right. Thank anyone who helps you. Then move on to the next thing. If you don't make a big deal about it, other people are likely to get past it quickly too. Just focus on moving forward and putting the mistake behind you.

What if people keep bringing up what you did wrong and teasing you about it, even long after it happened? You might want to just agree with them, in a neutral way. Obviously, don't agree if they're calling you names or being very nasty, but you could just calmly acknowledge the error.

Here are some possible responses. Try saying them in a slightly bored tone of voice.

* "Yep, I messed up."

* "Yeah, I didn't know how to do it then."

* "Uh-huh. That was a mistake."

* "You're right. I should have done it a different way."

* "I'll know better next time."

Notice that all of these comments acknowledge the blunder, but they don't involve putting yourself down. They're also not very interesting or satisfying for the teaser. This makes it less likely that the teasing will continue.

4

Feeling Guilty

COLLEEN'S CHALLENGE: SORRY ABOUT HER MISTAKE AND ANXIOUS ABOUT OTHERS' REACTIONS

Uh-oh, Colleen didn't mean to, but she hurt the other kid. The feeling she's having is called *guilt*. We feel *guilty* when we know we've done something wrong. Guilt is very uncomfortable, but it can actually be a healthy emotion because it helps us recognize when we are on the wrong path and need to move in a different direction.

Guilt helps people get along. Imagine if people did hurtful things and never felt bad about it. Yikes! Everyone would be hurting everyone all the time!

On the other hand, staying stuck feeling guilty all the time for everything we've ever done wrong isn't helpful. Colleen needs to figure out how to make up with the kid she hurt and move past her mistake so she can let go of her guilt.

> Guilt helps us recognize when we are on the wrong path and need to move in a different direction.

42

FEELINGS STORY: COLLEEN'S RESPONSE TO MAKING A MISTAKE

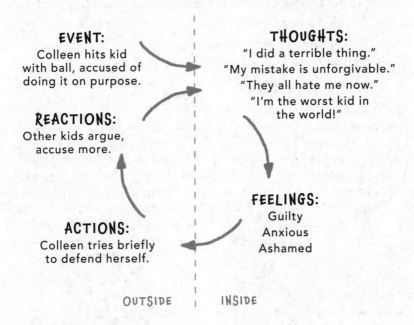

EVENT:
Colleen hits kid with ball, accused of doing it on purpose.

THOUGHTS:
"I did a terrible thing."
"My mistake is unforgivable."
"They all hate me now."
"I'm the worst kid in the world!"

REACTIONS:
Other kids argue, accuse more.

FEELINGS:
Guilty
Anxious
Ashamed

ACTIONS:
Colleen tries briefly to defend herself.

OUTSIDE | INSIDE

Colleen's Feelings Story begins with her accidentally hitting the other kid in the face with the kickball and being accused of doing it on purpose (events). She immediately starts thinking that she did a terrible thing, that everyone hates her, and that making this mistake is unforgivable. These thoughts lead her to feel guilty and probably also anxious about what the other kids will do or say.

There's another feeling that Colleen's thoughts lead her to feel, which is similar to guilt: it's shame. Guilt is about feeling bad because of what you did. **Shame** means feeling bad because you think you're a bad person. When Colleen thinks to herself, "I'm the worst kid in the world," that makes her feel **ashamed**. Like guilt, shame is an emotional warning sign that we need to change something, but shame is less useful than guilt because it can keep us stuck. It's hard to find a path forward if we believe we're totally bad!

Colleen tries briefly to defend herself (action), but that doesn't help. The other kids respond by arguing and continuing to accuse her (reaction). Poor Colleen doesn't know how to fix the relationship, so she's stuck believing that she made an unforgivable mistake and feeling even more guilty and ashamed. This doesn't help anyone.

Let's look at some ways to move beyond feeling guilty.

WHAT NOT TO SAY WHEN YOU'VE HURT SOMEONE (AND WHAT TO SAY INSTEAD)

When we've hurt someone, even if it was an accident, it's a good idea to apologize. This tells the person we've hurt that we care about them, and we regret doing it. Apologizing can also help ease guilt. But sometimes people have trouble apologizing well.

Here are some common but *unhelpful* ways to handle guilt. How do you think each of these will affect a friendship? Can you think of better ways to respond?

Unhelpful Choice:
Deny the Mistake or Make Excuses

Ugh. When we've done something wrong, it's very tempting to deny it and say we didn't do it. It's also tempting to offer a lot of excuses about why the mistake isn't our fault. But denying and making excuses don't help the person we've hurt feel better. In fact, if Colleen says she didn't do it, that's likely to lead to a "Yes, you did" / "No, I didn't" argument that goes nowhere and makes the injured kid feel even more mad.

It's difficult, but admitting what we did wrong is the best way to get past a misstep. Instead of arguing about whether and why the error happened, we can admit what we did and focus on how to make things better going forward. That's called *taking responsibility for our actions*. Grown-ups love it when kids do this. Other kids appreciate it too.

A Better Choice:
Offer a Sincere Apology

In this example, Colleen offers a sincere apology. She uses the words "I'm sorry *for*" and describes what she did that she regrets. Just saying "I'm sorry" without the "for" is not as powerful. In fact, just saying "Sorr-eeee!" can sound like you're not *really* sorry at all. Try to be clear and specific about what you regret doing so the other person knows you mean it.

Saying "I'm sorry, *but*..." is also not a good idea because that erases the apology. The other person will focus only on the part that comes after the "but," and the "I'm sorry" will disappear.

Another thing that Colleen does right in this example is she says what she should have done instead. That shows that she understands what she did wrong and wants to do better from now on.

Here's another not-so-good way to respond after hurting someone:

Unhelpful Choice:
Accuse Other People

Oh, dear. Feeling guilty is uncomfortable, so it's understandable that Colleen wants to pull the attention off of her and shift it onto other people by blaming everyone in sight. But blaming other people definitely doesn't help the person she hurt feel better! It's also likely to make all the people she accuses feel mad at her.

A Better Choice:
Try to Help

In this example, Colleen tries to make the situation better. After apologizing, it's a good idea to think about what the person you've hurt might need. This is a kind thing to do. Colleen offers three ideas of how she might be able to help her injured friend. Her friend may or may not want her to do those things, but offering is important. It shows Colleen cares.

Here's another example of an unhelpful response when you've hurt someone:

Unhelpful Choice: Make a Big, Dramatic Fuss about How You're Feeling

Ugh. Colleen hurt the other kid, but her comments focus only on herself. How many times did she say the word "I"? How many times does she say the word "you" in this example? How do you think that makes the other kid feel? Maybe like their feelings don't matter. Colleen is apologizing a lot, but she's not communicating that she cares about the kid she hurt.

Try not to apologize more than twice. The first "I'm sorry" tells someone you wish you hadn't hurt them. A second apology could be a way to show you really mean it. But more than two apologies shifts the attention away from the person you hurt and onto you. It might even make the person you hurt feel like they have to comfort you because you keep going on and on apologizing and talking about your feelings. That's backwards! The point of an apology is to help the other person feel better by showing we care about their feelings.

A Better Choice:
Keep the Focus on the Person Who Was Hurt

This response is a much better choice because Colleen is focusing on the needs of the kid who was hurt and what she might be able to do to help him. A good way to deal with guilt is to try to do what you can to make things right or at least move forward in a kinder direction.

FORGIVE YOURSELF TO LET GO OF GUILT

What if you've already apologized but you still feel guilty? It can be difficult, but it's also very important to let it go and forgive yourself. Guilt is a useful signal that you've made a mistake, but staying trapped in guilt doesn't help anyone. It's also not kind to yourself.

Dwelling on your mistakes can make them seem huge. It can be easier to forgive yourself if you put your mistake in *context*, meaning seeing it in comparison to everything else. Here are some questions that can help you do this:

Did you do it on purpose? Intentions matter. Remember, intentions are about what someone was trying to do. If you hurt someone without meaning to—because it was an accident, or you didn't realize they'd be upset, or even if you lashed out in the heat of the moment but you didn't really mean what you said—that's very different from planning to hurt someone on purpose. You didn't mean to be hurtful; it just happened. Yes, it was upsetting to the other person, but it was a mistake. Mistakes happen.

How bad was it, really? You wish you hadn't made the mistake, but was it really a life-changing mistake? A week or a month or a year from now, will it matter? Probably not. That doesn't mean you should keep making the same error, but it also doesn't make sense to have a huge amount of guilt for a small mistake.

Are you the only person who has ever done this? Everyone makes mistakes. That's part of being human. We're all sometimes careless or thoughtless. We say or do things that hurt people's feelings—even those we care about. Again, this doesn't give us permission to be mean, but if you did something that plenty of other people have done, maybe you can accept that you're human and move on.

What have you done to try to make things right? When we do something wrong, whenever possible, it's a good idea to do what we can to fix the situation. If you've apologized and tried to make things up to whoever you hurt, then it's probably time to let go of thinking about the past. What's done is done. You did what you could to fix the mistake.

What can you do differently from now on? This is the most important question. We're all constantly learning, and sometimes, unfortunately, we end up learning by doing it wrong first. So when you think about the bad thing that you did, don't focus on how bad it was or how bad you are! That's not useful. Instead, think about what you could do differently from now on. What could you do to prevent the problem? How might you respond differently the next time you're in that situation? What can you do now to make the situation better? Having a plan can help you let go of your guilt about the mistake.

But what if the mistake was unavoidable? If there's nothing you could do differently, recognizing that can help you move on. We can't erase the past. We can only move forward, as best we can.

After thinking honestly about these questions, you may want to think or write, "I forgive myself." This doesn't deny the mistake. It's giving yourself permission to let go of the guilt and move on.

Learning to look at yourself with kind eyes lets you move past mistakes. If you would forgive a friend for a certain mistake, chances are other people will forgive you. And even if they don't, you can forgive yourself. Staying stuck feeling guilty doesn't help anyone.

> Learning to look at yourself with kind eyes lets you move past mistakes.

52

5

The Opposites of Anxiety Are Excitement, Curiosity, and Playfulness

Feeling anxious about friends involves worrying about what-ifs. Anxiety makes us want to be careful and avoid danger. This can be useful, but it can also keep us stuck.

The four main kids that we talked about in part I each had fears about how other kids might react to them. They each did things to get rid of their feelings of anxiety that ended up either making them feel more anxious or hurting their relationships or both. Luis wanted to avoid his friend's birthday party, Violet kept messaging her friend and looking for reassurance, Jaleel wanted to hide from positive attention, and Colleen fretted and beat herself up over her mistake. For each of them, their Feelings Stories—the around-and-around pattern of their thoughts, feelings, and actions—kept them stuck, feeling more and more anxious.

We've talked about lots of ways that these kids could change their thoughts and actions in order to change their feelings. We looked at ways they could shift their ideas about their situations so they'd seem less scary. We also looked at ways they could do something—even though they felt scared—to lower their anxiety and strengthen their relationships. For Luis, this meant going to the party; for Violet it was trusting her friend; for

Jaleel it was getting used to attention by actually seeking it out; and for Colleen, it was offering a genuine apology and letting herself move forward in kind ways. Doing something even though you feel scared is the definition of bravery.

There's also another way to ease anxious feelings, and that's by focusing on the **Opposite Feelings**. The opposite of anxiety isn't boring calmness; it's feelings like excitement, curiosity, and playfulness. These are all forms of happiness. **Happiness** means having positive, enjoyable feelings. **Excitement** is when you're eagerly looking forward to something. You might feel all jittery inside, but it's a fun jitteriness. **Curiosity** is the feeling when you wonder and want to discover. **Playful** means feeling silly and lighthearted.

Anxiety tells us to be careful and watch out for danger. That can be useful sometimes. But those Opposite Feelings are what pull us forward, helping us grow and deepen our friendships. Opposite Feelings can balance out and sometimes even replace anxious feelings. They are different kinds of happiness that you can experience at the same time as anxiety.

When you're feeling anxious about friends, looking *within yourself* for those opposite, moving-forward feelings can help you ease the anxiety.

Can you think of a time when you were nervous about doing something, but you did it anyway because you also felt **excited** or **curious**? Do you remember a time when you felt anxious, but your friend said or did something silly, and you ended up laughing together?

Looking for the Opposite Feelings, even or especially when you're feeling anxious, is about choosing how you want to be in the world. Opposite Feelings give you the energy to do what you want to do, even if you're scared.

Look how these kids are using moving-forward, Opposite Feelings to manage their anxious feelings:

Excitement

Curiosity

Playfulness

What do you want to learn or try or experience? Go for it! Walk through that door! Focus on the curiosity and excitement that pull you forward rather than the anxiety that holds you back.

Instead of imagining everything that could go wrong (which feeds anxiety) think about what you want so you can move toward it. Give those Opposite Feelings a louder voice in your head than the anxiety's voice. There's a whole wide world to explore and lots of fun to be had with friends when you don't let anxiety keep you stuck!

> Instead of imagining everything that could go wrong, think about what you want.

57

THINK ABOUT IT!

Here are some questions to help you think about dealing with feeling anxious about friends:

* Why do you think kids often feel nervous about going to events or activities where they don't know any other kids? What advice would you give those kids?

* Can you think of a time when you spoke with someone you didn't know, and you ended up becoming friends? How did that happen?

* What is a problem with friends that you worried about that actually *didn't* happen? Did worrying about it help prevent it or just make you feel worse?

* Do you remember a situation where you felt embarrassed around other kids? What happened? How long did your embarrassment last? Do you think anyone else remembers what happened?

* Can you think of an activity with friends or other kids that you'd like to do but you're scared to try? What are some baby steps you could do to start building up your confidence that you can handle it?

* Have you ever made a big mistake with a friend that you felt guilty about? How did you move past it? Have you ever felt very hurt by a friend's mistake? Did that mistake end the friendship or were you able to move on? What did your friend do that made it harder or easier to stay friends?

Wow! I'm learning a lot from this book.

I didn't know you had stage fright.

I would like to get over anxiety from stage fright by standing in front of a giant audience that is gathered to admire my long and lovely whiskers.

I don't, but let's gather a giant audience for me anyway!

PART II
Feeling Angry about Friends

Cats are very good at handling anger. We're natural predators. We pounce, we hiss, we swipe, we bite. . . . Problem solved!

I don't think that's so helpful with friends.

Anger is the emotion we feel when we believe we're being blocked from what we want to do or we're being treated unfairly. Feeling **angry** with friends comes up when they do things that we don't like or that we believe are hurtful to us.

Sometimes kids think it's bad to be angry. It's true that anger can be expressed in ways that are scary or destructive, but that's about actions not feelings. Feelings are never dangerous. Anger is actually a useful signal. It tells us, "This isn't right!" It can give us the energy to stand up for ourselves or get through challenging situations. Here are some ideas to help you deal with feeling angry with friends.

6
Feeling Furious

BAO'S CHALLENGE: ARGUING WITH A FRIEND

Bao is feeling furious because his friend ruined his hard work. *Furious* is an intense form of anger. When you're furious, it can feel like you're going to explode with anger. Sometimes people do things they later regret when they're feeling furious.

Anyone would feel mad in Bao's situation! But then what happens? He speaks up right away about the problem: "Hey, you wrecked my building!" Bringing up an issue right when it happens can be a good way to solve things, but then Bao and Jeffrey get into a big argument about who was cheating, and Bao ends up throwing the controller. That's not a helpful response.

Often what leads kids to feel angry about friends is their sense that something is unfair. Bao thinks it's unfair that Jeffrey broke his building, so he may believe that makes it OK for him to break Jeffrey's controller. But it's not Bao's job to punish Jeffrey or decide what Jeffrey deserves. Nobody elected him as judge.

> Often what leads kids to feel angry about friends is their sense that something is unfair.

64

FEELINGS STORY:
BAO'S RESPONSE TO JEFFREY
BREAKING HIS VIDEO GAME BUILDING

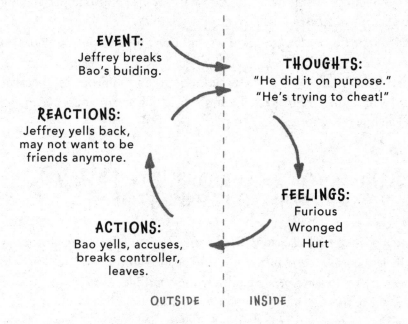

EVENT:
Jeffrey breaks
Bao's buiding.

THOUGHTS:
"He did it on purpose."
"He's trying to cheat!"

REACTIONS:
Jeffrey yells back,
may not want to be
friends anymore.

FEELINGS:
Furious
Wronged
Hurt

ACTIONS:
Bao yells, accuses,
breaks controller,
leaves.

OUTSIDE | INSIDE

Can you see how Bao's thoughts, feelings, and actions create his Feelings Story? The starting event is Jeffrey breaking his building. Bao thinks Jeffrey did it on purpose in order to cheat at the game. This makes Bao feel furious. He also feels **wronged**, which means angry because something seems unfair. And, he may feel hurt because it was his friend who wrecked his building. Often, when people are angry, they also feel hurt. He responds to those feelings by doing something mean back to Jeffrey. This is likely to lead to more mean behavior from Jeffrey, which will make Bao feel even angrier.

How do you think Jeffrey feels about what Bao did? From Jeffrey's point of view, Bao breaking the controller probably seemed very mean and much worse than breaking something in a video game. Bao's actions spread his anger to Jeffrey, and they may lead Jeffrey to not want to be friends with Bao anymore.

Bao and Jeffrey are experiencing something called escalation. *Escalation* is when a situation gets worse and worse. Upset feelings can get bigger and bigger, like a snowball growing and gathering more and more snow as it rolls down a hill. In this case, both boys' actions contribute to making their argument **escalate**.

Have you heard the phrase "Two wrongs don't make a right"? What do you think that means?

It means that it's not OK to do something mean to someone just because they did something mean first. Doing something mean . . . is mean, no matter what came before.

WHEN YOU'RE FURIOUS, STEP AWAY AND WAIT OUT THE STORM

We rarely make good decisions when we're furious. Bao's stepping away from the game was a good move; it just happened a little too late. It would have been better to leave *before* he threw the controller.

When we're furious, it's very tempting to lash out and try to hurt others the way they've hurt us. This definitely doesn't help anyone. It makes the conflict worse, and it could end a friendship. Maybe Bao will make up his mind that he doesn't want to be friends with Jeffrey anymore, but he shouldn't decide this in the heat of the moment.

What if Bao had said, "I'm so mad that you wrecked my building! I need to stop playing for now"? That might have prevented things from getting worse. Stepping away when we're furious is very difficult, but if we do it as soon as we notice our temper starting to flare—especially if we can do it before things get too heated—we give ourselves some room to calm down and think about what we want to do next.

Very intense feelings are like a storm. Have you ever watched a thunderstorm? For a few minutes, the clouds are rumbling, lightning is flashing, rain is pounding, and the wind is roaring. Then what happens? The storm passes, and everything eases up and quiets down.

Bao says he's going home. If that's not possible, he could step away from the situation by going to the bathroom or getting a drink of water, to let the storm of his anger pass.

TRY SOME CALMING STRATEGIES

If you're ever in a situation where you feel furiously angry, you may want to try using some ***Emergency First Aid Calming Strategies***. These are quick strategies to use in the moment with friends, not to solve a problem, but just to help yourself calm down so you can think. Here are some possibilities:

* **Breathe out, long and slow.** Keep breathing out until you feel your belly going in. Breathe in and repeat until you feel calmer.

* **Do math facts in your head.** Maybe count up by threes or figure out 100 minus 7, then minus 7 from that, then minus 7 from that . . .

* **Notice five things.** Try noticing five things that are blue, or five things that begin with *s*, or five things that are round.

* **Give yourself a little hug** by crossing your arms.

* **Splash your face** with cool water.

If you can leave the upsetting situation, that can give you the chance to take a longer break to calm down. You could try reading a book, going for a walk outside, watching TV, eating a snack, or chatting with a friend or family member about something else.

The things that definitely *won't* help you calm down are yelling or punching pillows. Those just keep you riled up as you go over and over in your mind whatever upset you. The best way to become an angry person is to practice, practice, practice being angry! During your break, do things that are *not* related to feeling angry so your mind can rest.

Distracting yourself when you're angry gives you time and space to let your feelings settle down. Then, when you're feeling calmer, you'll be better able to think about how to solve the problem.

IMAGINE THE GOOD OR NEUTRAL REASONS FOR BAD BEHAVIOR

Friends are human. That means they often do things we don't like. In Bao's case, he felt mad at Jeffrey, not just because his building was wrecked, but because he assumed that Jeffrey broke it on purpose in order to cheat. How would Bao have felt if he knew it was an accident? He'd probably still be annoyed that the building was broken, but he wouldn't be furious at Jeffrey.

People who frequently get mad tend to assume that other people do things because they're trying to be mean. That's actually pretty rare. Most of the time, when friends do something we don't like, it's just a mistake or a misunderstanding. If you can think of other reasons for a friend's actions—besides trying to be mean—you're more likely to come up with the truth, avoid unnecessary anger, and keep your friendships.

Here are two examples of kids who are mad about something their friends did. Can you think of some possible good or neutral reasons behind their friends' upsetting behaviors? A good intention means the friend was trying to be kind. A neutral intention means it just happened—the person wasn't trying to be either kind or unkind, and it wasn't caused by anything related to the friendship.

Wait, wait, wait! Don't be so fast to decide what the friend is trying to do. What are some other reasons why his friend might have gotten those shoes, besides trying to be mean?

* Maybe his friend's dad bought the shoes, not even knowing that he had them.

* Maybe his friend admires his style and thinks copying him is a compliment.

* Maybe those were the only shoes at the store that fit his friend's feet.

* Maybe his friend bought the shoes before he did!

That's a hard one. No one likes to have their secrets spread, but it's still worth thinking about other reasons why this might have happened, besides that the friend was trying to be mean. Can you think of some?

* Maybe her friend didn't realize she wanted that information kept private.

* Maybe her friend just kind of accidentally blurted it out and feels bad about that now.

* Maybe her friend thought the other person already knew the secret.

* Maybe it wasn't this friend who told the secret.

When you can imagine all the other reasons a friend might have done something, it makes the explanation that they were trying to be mean seem less likely, and it makes it easier to let go of the anger.

THINK ABOUT YOUR ROLE IN THE PROBLEM

Our eyes point outward, so it's easy to notice when someone else is doing something wrong. It's much more difficult to see what we might have done wrong or how we might have contributed to a friendship problem. Especially when we're angry, we may find it more comfortable to focus on whatever bad thing our friend did. But if a friendship is struggling, it's rarely just one person who is responsible for that. Figuring out what we could do differently can be very useful.

Sometimes you can figure out your role in the problem by asking yourself, "What happened before that? And before that? And before that?" By tracing back the chain of events, you may be able to see how you played a part in the conflict or unhappy event. This is not about blaming yourself or anyone. It's about trying to figure out how to move forward in better ways.

In Bao's case, his part in the conflict included throwing the controller, but there might be more. Jeffrey mentioned that Bao changed the rules to favor himself "again." Out of caring for Jeffrey, Bao may need to think about what he does that makes Jeffrey think he's not playing fairly. He may be tempted to make excuses for himself along the lines of "Well, Jeffrey does it too!" or "He did something worse last week!" That's not helpful.

Thinking about your role in the problem isn't about deciding who is bad or worse. And it's definitely not about being harsh or mean to yourself. It's about looking at what you can control—your own actions—to build a better friendship.

OFFER AN APOLOGY AND MAKE AMENDS

If you figure out you did something that wasn't kind, the right thing to do is to apologize. A sincere apology is often the fastest way to make up with a friend. Say, "I'm sorry for . . ." and mention what you did that you regret. Then, to show you really mean the apology, try to make amends. *Making amends* happens after you've done something wrong, and it means doing what you can to make the situation right, either now or in the future.

In Bao's case, he might decide to tell Jeffrey, "I'm very sorry for changing the rules in the middle of the game and for throwing your controller. I'll be more careful with your stuff from now on." He could also get Jeffrey a new controller to replace the one he broke.

In order to genuinely apologize, you need to be able to imagine your friend's point of view. It's not always easy or comfortable to do this. You can start by remembering times when you've been in a similar situation. But you also need to use what you know about your friend to help you imagine their reactions.

Imagining a friend's point of view is not about deciding who is right. You can both be right, even when you see things differently.

Have you heard the old story about three blindfolded people describing an elephant? One touches the trunk and says, "It's like a thick snake!" Another touches the elephant's side and says, "It's like a wall!" A third touches the tail and says, "It's like a rope!" Who's right? They're all partly right, but the whole truth is a combination of their experiences.

Here are two examples of kids who are making an effort to understand their friends' points of view. Neither kid intended to hurt their friend, and they can both see how, from their friends' points of view, their actions were hurtful.

It's important to keep in mind that if you apologize to someone, even if you really mean it and do everything you can to make things right, the other person may not accept your apology, and they may not apologize back to you. You can't control what other people do, but you'll know you did the right thing by apologizing.

DECIDE WHETHER TO TALK ABOUT THE PROBLEM OR MOVE FORWARD IN OTHER WAYS

When you and a friend have a conflict where you get very mad at each other, it's important to think wisely about the best way to move past that conflict. Sometimes, especially when it's a big problem that keeps happening, it's important to talk with your friend about what's going on, but that's not your only option. Here are some other possibilities:

Reconnect with fun. Often, the way kids get past a Friendship Rough Spot is to separate for a bit, so tempers can cool, and then get back together again and just have fun. Having a good time with your friend reminds you both what you enjoy about each other, and it shows a willingness to forgive each other and let go of whatever the problem was before.

Change what you do from now on. If you did the work of thinking about your role in the problem, you may have some ideas of what you could do differently the next time the difficult situation comes up. This might mean communicating better in the moment, reacting differently, or accepting your friend as they are, just because you care about that friend.

> Think wisely about the best way to move past the conflict.

Sometimes, if you change how you act, the other person will change how they respond, and the friendship will improve.

Change the situation. You may decide that the best way to deal with a difficult situation with a friend is to change that situation. For instance, if Bao and Jeffrey usually end up arguing when they play video games, it might make sense for them to find something else to do together. Maybe they could ride bikes, or play a board game, or make mug cakes in the microwave. . . . Any of these activities could

75

help them enjoy each other's company while staying away from situations that bring out the worst in them.

SPEAK UP IN A WAY THAT YOU'RE MORE LIKELY TO BE HEARD

If you decide to speak with your friend about the problem that made you feel mad, try to do it in a way that makes it easier for your friend to listen. Aim to be honest and also kind.

Have you ever worked on a project with someone, maybe even a friend, who didn't help by doing their part? That's very frustrating, and it's not fair, but how you handle it can make a big difference in how the other person reacts. Here are two examples of how to speak up about that problem. Which approach do you think is likely to get a better response from the project partner?

If you picked the second box, you're right!

The comments in the first box include a lot of things that shut down listening, including the words *always* and *never*, which make the listener want to argue. They involve name-calling, which hardly ever goes anywhere good. And they don't offer any suggestion of how to move forward. It's very unlikely that the project partner will hear these and think, "I'd like to help!" The partner will probably just think, "Ugh! Get me out of here!"

The comments in the second box are polite. They state the facts, clearly describing the kid's efforts, and they ask directly for help.

When we're frustrated, it's easy to accuse, blame, and focus only on how wrong the other person is. But to move forward, we want to communicate in a way that's likely to get the response we want. The comments in the second box don't guarantee that the project partner will help, but the polite request makes it easier for the partner to understand and respond well.

KNOW WHEN TO MOVE ON

Sometimes your anger with a friend is just a temporary frustration that you can get past. But sometimes, your anger is a sign that it's time to say goodbye to a friendship.

Friendships are precious, so you don't want to throw them away easily, but here are some questions to consider if you're wondering whether to end a friendship.

IS A FRIENDSHIP WORTH CONTINUING?

* How do you feel most of the time when you're with this friend?

* Do you and your friend argue more than you have fun?

* Have you tried talking in a kind way to your friend about what you want?

* Does your friend usually care about your feelings?

* Is your friend genuinely sorry after making a mistake?

* If your friend doesn't change, can you accept your friend even if they do things you don't like?

* Are you doing what you can to be a good friend?

If you've done what you can to try to improve the friendship, and you still mostly feel bad when you're with this friend, it's probably time to move on.

You don't have to make a big announcement like "Our friendship is over!" or "I'm never speaking to you again!" You definitely should not talk badly about your old friend to other people. That's not kind. Instead, just start spending more time with other kids. If you see your old friend at school or in a large group, you don't have to run away! You can be polite. Just put more of your time and energy into friendships that make you feel good.

79

7
Feeling Jealous

MIRIAM'S CHALLENGE:
MAD ABOUT BEING LEFT OUT

Mad is a kind of angry feeling that is directed at a certain person or thing. Miriam is mad at Anika for getting together with Eva without her. She's also feeling *jealous* of Eva. *Jealousy* about friends is the feeling that comes up when we believe another person might hurt or even break up our close friendship. Miriam believes that Eva is stealing her friend Anika.

FEELINGS STORY: MIRIAM'S RESPONSE TO ANIKA GETTING TOGETHER WITH EVA

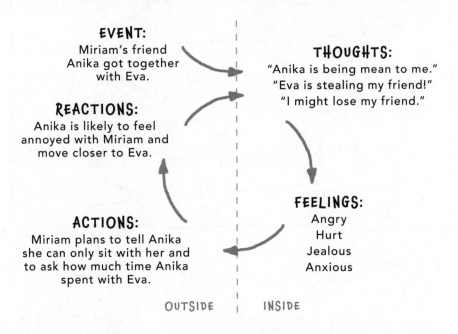

EVENT:
Miriam's friend Anika got together with Eva.

THOUGHTS:
"Anika is being mean to me."
"Eva is stealing my friend!"
"I might lose my friend."

REACTIONS:
Anika is likely to feel annoyed with Miriam and move closer to Eva.

FEELINGS:
Angry
Hurt
Jealous
Anxious

ACTIONS:
Miriam plans to tell Anika she can only sit with her and to ask how much time Anika spent with Eva.

OUTSIDE | INSIDE

Let's think about Miriam's Feelings Story: The starting event is finding out that her buddy Anika got together with Eva without her. The story Miriam creates with her thoughts about this event is that Anika is being mean to her and that Eva is stealing her friend. These thoughts lead Miriam to feel a bunch of emotions: She's angry at Anika and probably also feeling hurt because she thinks Anika having other friends means Anika doesn't care as much about her. She's jealous of Eva and anxious that her friendship with Anika might end. Then, moving to actions, Miriam decides to try to make her uncomfortable feelings go away by trying to control Anika. She plans to say that Anika has to sit by her, and not Eva, at lunch. She also wants to quiz Anika about how much time she spent with Eva, checking to make sure that Eva doesn't get more time with Anika than she does. That probably won't work out well. Miriam senses that Anika is pulling away from her and moving toward Eva, but these actions could end up annoying Anika, who might decide she'd rather hang out with Eva because of what Miriam does.

AVOID KEEPING SCORE

Miriam is having a *Keeping-Score Mindset* with her friend Anika. This mindset means always being on the lookout for anything that might be unfair to you.

Keeping-Score Mindset

A Keeping-Score Mindset involves constantly comparing your situation to other people's situations. Did they get more than you? Did they get something you didn't? Did they do exactly the same amount of work as you did? Was their work easier than what you had to do? Did they get away with doing something you're not allowed to do?

This mindset makes kids angry and jealous because life is *never* completely fair. If you're always looking for unfairness, you will definitely find it, and you'll miss out on good things happening. It's also not caring or generous to be concerned only about how things affect you.

Friendship is not a place for a Keeping-Score Mindset. Miriam is treating Anika like she's a birthday cake, by trying to divide her up and worrying about who gets a bigger piece. That's not kind to Anika. And it doesn't make sense.

A Friend Is Not a Birthday Cake That You Can Divide into Pieces

Anika is allowed to have more than one friend. She is not doing anything wrong by getting together with Eva. Miriam needs to accept that. Miriam will also get a much better response from Anika if she focuses on being kind and having fun together instead of trying to tell Anika who she's allowed to play with and for how long.

> If you're always looking for unfairness, you will definitely find it.

If you have a situation where you feel jealous about a friend, try to remind yourself that it's generous and caring to accept your friend's other friendships with good grace. Showing your friend that you are generous and caring helps your friendship continue and maybe even grow closer.

SOFTENING YOUR "SHOULDS"

"Should" is a harsh word, especially in a friendship. It tends to lead to anger. You may have strong opinions about what your friend should or shouldn't do. But just because you would do something one way, and you think it's better than what your friend does, that doesn't mean your friend *has* to do it that way. You're not the boss of your friend.

Look at these two kids. One is stuck thinking about how things should be in a perfect world. The other recognizes a preference. A **preference** means when you notice that you'd rather have one situation instead of another, but you know you can deal with whatever happens.

85

Neither of these kids can control the weather. Which one is in a better frame of mind to have a good day? If you guessed the second kid, you're right! The "I'd prefer" gives this kid room to make different plans instead of being stuck, thinking about what isn't going right.

If you find yourself thinking in "shoulds," try swapping them in your mind for the phrase "I'd prefer." Here are some examples. How could you rewrite each kid's "should" as an "I'd prefer"?

Ooh! This kid is thinking just like Miriam. How could he replace his "should" with an "I'd prefer"? Maybe: "I'd prefer that Esteban invite me." Wow, that just drains the anger and leaves plenty of room to do something fun on his own or with someone else.

Now, try another one:

Well, it makes sense that this girl wouldn't like her friend talking about her behind her back, but that's not something she can control. How could she soften her "should" to an "I'd prefer"? How about: "I'd prefer that she didn't talk about me when I'm not around"? That's a good one! She'd definitely rather not be the topic of her friend's conversation, but she's going to move on and live her life, even if things don't go exactly how she wants.

Do you hear the softening in these examples? "I'd prefer" captures what you want, but it also recognizes that people don't always do what we want. Thinking "I'd prefer" helps you accept that. On the other hand, focusing on "shoulds" keeps you stuck in anger.

KEEP YOUR FRIENDSHIP BAG OF MARBLES FULL

A friendship is kind of like a bag of marbles. Whenever you and your friend have good times together, it's like you're adding a marble to your *Friendship Bag of Marbles* and strengthening the friendship. A full bag means a strong friendship with that person. Doing something kind or helpful for a friend, giving the friend a sincere compliment, having fun together . . . little by little, these actions (like marbles) help your friendship grow (to a full bag).

> Kind actions build up friendships slowly, but unkind actions drain a friendship very quickly.

On the other hand, arguing or yelling at your friend, saying or doing mean things like ignoring them, gossiping about them, or lying to or about a friend, even hurting or breaking your friend's things, are all examples of actions that take marbles away from your Friendship Bag of Marbles. Yikes! All of these examples are like ripping a big hole in the Friendship Bag of Marbles, and the marbles would quickly pour out.

This is something very important that a lot of kids don't realize: kind actions build up friendships slowly, but unkind actions drain a friendship very quickly.

Kind Actions Build a Friendship Bit by Bit

Unkind Actions Drain a Friendship Very Quickly

In other words, if you and a friend have about the same amount of good times and bad times, your friendship is not likely to last. Those bad times will drain the friendship faster than the good times can build it. If you want your friendship to grow, you need to have lots and lots of kind actions and very, very few friendship-draining, unkind acts. That way the kind actions will far outweigh the unkind ones, and your friendship is more likely to last.

EASE JEALOUSY WITH ACCEPTANCE, WARMTH, AND OPENNESS

Miriam is trying to get rid of her feelings of jealousy by checking on and trying to control her friend Anika. It's easy to imagine how those actions could lead Anika to want to hang out more with Eva, just to avoid all that unpleasantness.

But these feelings are very painful! What could Miriam do instead? Here are three ideas, which are not easy, but are her best bet for keeping her friendship with Anika.

Accept that we can't control what friends do. Miriam thinks she has to *do* something to hold on tightly to Anika so Eva doesn't steal her. That thought isn't true, and it isn't helpful. It's hard, but Anika needs to accept that we can't *make* someone be our friend. Friendships sometimes end just because people grow apart.

Miriam also needs to accept that Anika will make her own choices about who she wants to be friends with. That's just the way life works. If the worst happens and she and Anika do have a friendship breakup, Miriam will survive and move on to new friendships herself. But right now, they're friends.

Express warm feelings. Telling Anika, "You're mean!" or "You're not being fair!" is not going to make her feel good or want to hang out with Miriam. Those comments criticize Anika, saying she's bad.

90

On the other hand, saying, "I miss spending time with you" or "Let's get together this weekend!" or even "I like playing with you!" are all warm, caring words that are about enjoying being with her. They strengthen the friendship and are likely to lead Anika to feel good about spending time with Miriam.

Be open to new friendships. What if, instead of seeing Eva as someone who is trying to steal her friend, Miriam decided to be open to getting to know Eva better? They both like Anika, so they already have something in common! Anika likes Eva, so by being interested in getting to know and maybe even becoming friends with Eva, Miriam would be responding in a caring way to Anika's feelings.

Friendship threesomes can be difficult. If you think of a triangle connecting three friends, it's hard to keep all three sides equal at all times. Often, a good strategy in this situation is to expand the triangle by inviting a fourth or even a fifth or sixth friend into the group. A bigger friendship group can increase the fun and also make it easier to get along.

Developing other friendships beyond Anika and Eva could help Miriam be a better friend to Anika. She might feel less jealous if she also has other choices of people to hang out with. And, if the friendship with Anika does run into trouble, Miriam would have an easier time dealing with that if she already has other friends.

8

Feeling Irritated and Mean

LOLA'S CHALLENGE: HATING SOMEONE'S GUTS

Feeling *irritated* is a low-level anger when someone or something just bothers us. In Lola's case, not only is she irritated by Penelope, but she's also feeling *mean*—she wants to hurt or get back at Penelope by making the other girls at her lunch table also dislike Penelope.

Lola and Penelope have a history. They used to be friends, but now that friendship is over. That happens. But Lola is still very involved with Penelope in a negative way. She considers Penelope her enemy. She's constantly watching Penelope and—worse—saying mean things about her to other people. *Enemy Thinking* means spending a lot of energy watching, judging, and even plotting against someone you strongly dislike.

But what if it's true? Maybe Penelope really did blab Lola's secrets! Maybe she really does have an annoying laugh!

Enemy Thinking can be exciting. It adds drama to the day. It gives you something to talk about or even laugh about with other kids as you're watching and wondering, "What's the enemy going to do next?!"

But treating someone as an enemy is not kind. Enemy Thinking also keeps you stuck feeling angry, and it tends to build up and make situations worse.

Enemy Thinking keeps you stuck feeling angry.

FEELINGS STORY:
LOLA'S RESPONSE TO SEEING
PENELOPE AND HEARING HER LAUGH

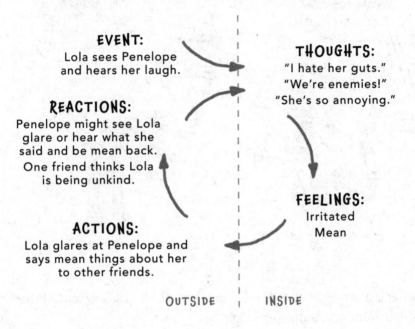

EVENT:
Lola sees Penelope
and hears her laugh.

THOUGHTS:
"I hate her guts."
"We're enemies!"
"She's so annoying."

REACTIONS:
Penelope might see Lola
glare or hear what she
said and be mean back.
One friend thinks Lola
is being unkind.

ACTIONS:
Lola glares at Penelope and
says mean things about her
to other friends.

FEELINGS:
Irritated
Mean

OUTSIDE | INSIDE

Let's think about Lola's Feelings Story. The story between them started a while ago, with the breakup of their friendship, but the event that sets things in motion now is Lola just seeing Penelope and hearing her laugh. Other people might hear Penelope's laugh and not be bothered at all. But the meaning that Lola's thoughts attach to that event—about Penelope being her enemy and being annoying—makes Lola feel irritated and mean. She wants to hurt Penelope. It's possible that she might also be experiencing some hurt feelings that are left over from their old argument.

Lola's actions involve glaring at Penelope and saying mean things about her to other friends. If Penelope notices this, she might react by saying mean things about Lola, adding to the "war" between them. Enemy Thinking can easily lead to escalation and make problems much worse.

WHATEVER YOU PUT OUT INTO THE WORLD IS WHAT YOU TEND TO GET BACK

If you do something mean to someone, how are they likely to respond? They'll probably do something mean back! And then you'll do something meaner. And then they'll do something meaner. And you'll end up doing very mean stuff that you never would have believed you'd do plus getting hurt in return. On the other hand, if you are kind to others, there's a good chance that they'll be kind back to you. It's worth a try.

What Are You Putting Out into the World?

Here's another reason to avoid Enemy Thinking: it can hurt how people view you. One friend, Amy, was laughing and agreeing with Lola, but the other girl, even though she didn't say anything, thought Lola and Amy were being mean.

The third girl was probably also thinking, "If Lola talks like this about Penelope, she could do the same thing to me!" No one will ever think, "Oooh! I want to be friends with Lola because she's so nasty to Penelope!" In trying to attack Penelope, Lola might end up hurting herself by pushing other friends away.

And what do you think would happen if a teacher heard Lola's comments? Lola could get in big trouble.

You don't have to like everyone, but it's not right to be deliberately mean to anyone. And encouraging other people to be mean to someone makes you a bully. Don't go there.

WATCH OUT FOR EXCUSES

Sometimes kids decide that certain people's feelings don't count, so it's OK to be mean to them. Maybe those people do annoying things or did something mean in the past. Maybe they're younger or look different or get picked on by lots of other people.

None of those excuses matter. An *excuse* is an argument that tries to explain away some wrong action by saying it's not really wrong. People make excuses when they don't want to look bad, but excuses don't help people move forward in a good way.

You know what's right. You know what's kind. You know what you should do. Be careful not to let excuses get in the way of doing the right thing with friends or other kids. If you would feel embarrassed if your parent or a teacher knew that you did something, that usually means you shouldn't do it.

> You know what's right. You know what's kind. You know what you should do.

EASE AWAY FROM ENEMY THINKING

But what if Lola really, really, *really* doesn't like Penelope? Then she shouldn't give Penelope that much space in her life. If she's constantly watching and talking about Penelope, she's keeping herself upset and making Penelope too important.

Lola doesn't have to make a show of avoiding Penelope or refusing to speak with her. That would keep the Enemy Thinking going. Instead, she can treat her with the same politeness she would treat someone she doesn't know well.

If Penelope is currently doing something mean to Lola and Lola has asked her to stop but it hasn't helped, it may be a good idea to tell an adult. But if there's nothing serious happening now, the best bet may be for Lola to change how she thinks and acts toward Penelope.

Instead of dwelling on Penelope's "badness," Lola could focus on taking care of herself by easing away from Enemy Thinking. Here are some things she could say to herself:

* "I've moved on. I don't have to keep thinking and talking about what happened."

* "I can't control what she does: I can only choose what I do."

* "I can choose to forgive her, even if she hasn't apologized, just because I don't want to keep carrying that anger toward her."

* "I have more interesting things to talk about with my friends than complaining about her."

* "Next year, I probably won't even remember that she did this. It won't matter."

* "I don't like her, but I'm a good person, so I'm not going to be mean."

Notice that none of these thoughts are about Lola trying to convince herself that Penelope is great. They're not even about Penelope. They're about Lola reminding herself how she wants to be in the world.

9
Feeling Grumpy

**RAJ'S CHALLENGE:
SNAPPING AT A FRIEND BECAUSE
HE'S HAVING A BAD DAY**

Raj is definitely having a bad day. He is feeling *grumpy*, which means bothered and a little bit angry about everything. It would have been nice if his friend noticed that he looked grumpy and asked what was going on, but Raj didn't say anything, so the friend didn't know. His friend was just thinking about the bus ride and eating a snack.

Let's take a look at Raj's Feelings Story.

FEELINGS STORY: RAJ'S RESPONSE TO A FRIEND OFFERING HIM POPCORN

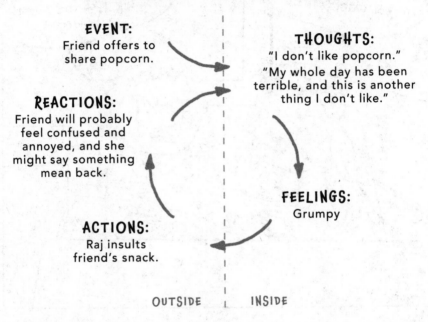

EVENT:
Friend offers to
share popcorn.

THOUGHTS:
"I don't like popcorn."
"My whole day has been
terrible, and this is another
thing I don't like."

REACTIONS:
Friend will probably
feel confused and
annoyed, and she
might say something
mean back.

FEELINGS:
Grumpy

ACTIONS:
Raj insults
friend's snack.

OUTSIDE | INSIDE

The event that gets things going is Raj's friend offering to share her popcorn. This was a kind thing for his friend to do, but Raj's thoughts make him see it as just another rotten event on a rotten day, which adds to his grumpy feelings.

Then, moving to action, Raj takes his grumpy mood out on his friend and calls her snack stupid.

Ugh. How is Raj's friend likely to respond to this insult? Not well. By snapping at his friend—who had nothing to do with the indoor recess or the spelling sentences—Raj is spreading his grumpiness. He's being mean to his friend. The friend will probably feel confused and annoyed, and she might respond by saying something mean back. This would make Raj feel even more grumpy! Insulting his friend doesn't help Raj's mood, and it's not pleasant for his friend either.

But wait! Raj has plenty of reasons to feel grumpy! Indoor recess, a drippy sandwich, and ten spelling sentences could put anyone in a bad mood! If he really is feeling grumpy, is he supposed to be fake and pretend that he's cheerful?

Of course not! Being kind and polite to others even though you're feeling grumpy is not the same as being fake. Being fake is about trying to trick or hurt others. Being fake involves being nice to someone in person and then turning around and saying nasty things behind their back. Treating others well, even when we're feeling grumpy, isn't being fake; it's being kind.

Let's look at some things you can do when you're feeling grumpy that won't hurt your friendships.

> Treating others well, even when we're feeling grumpy, isn't being fake; it's being kind.

BRING YOUR BEST SELF TO THE PARTY

Sometimes kids say they can't help acting grumpy when they feel grumpy. This is not true. It's harder to be pleasant to others when we're feeling out of sorts, but we always have a choice in how we act. And we're all responsible for creating a peaceful world.

Trying to be kind to others when we feel grumpy can be difficult, but it's possible, and you'll probably feel good about doing it. You can think of it as bringing your best self to the party, wherever you are.

Bring Your Best Self to the Party

Uh-oh. That third kid ruined it for everyone! That's not kind!

Bringing your best self to the party means doing your part to make whatever situation you're in better, not worse.

Bringing your best self is about digging deep, past your own grumpiness, and genuinely caring about others. It's about recognizing that how we treat others affects them. If you're nasty to others, they're going to feel worse. They're also likely to do to you what you just did to them. Ugh! Then you'd be stuck in a whole escalating contest of who can be grumpiest, and you'd both be feeling really upset and hurt.

Don't sign up for a grumpiness contest! Tell yourself, "I'm not going to take my mood out on other people!" Choosing to be kind prevents grumpiness from spreading. You have the power to spread joy and happiness. And here's a side benefit: being kind to others is likely to help you feel less grumpy!

If you know the other person well, you may want to tell them how you're feeling and why, but be sure your actions and tone of voice are kind. For instance, instead of snapping at his friend, Raj could have said, "No, thanks." Then maybe he could have told his friend, "I'm having a rough day." The friend probably would have responded in a caring way.

TRY TO SAY THE MOST MAGICAL WORD EVER

What do you think is the most magical word ever?

Some kids guess "Please" or "Thanks" or "Love." These are all very magical, but the most magical word ever is . . .

Saying "OK" shows you're willing to listen and get along. It's like a soft blanket, keeping relationships cozy. It's also a great way to move past grumpiness.

Here are two different ways someone could respond to a request from a friend. Which response do you think is better? Why?

Response One

Response Two

If you guessed the kid in the second box, you're right! The kid in the first box is likely to spark a big argument. But that simple "OK" from the kid in the second box sends the conversation in a much better direction.

Obviously, you have to say "OK" in a friendly or at least calm way. Yelling "OK!" doesn't help. But when you say "OK"—and mean it—you're telling the other person that you're willing to move forward in a peaceful direction. Yay, you!

Does this mean that Raj has to say "OK" and eat popcorn that he doesn't like? Of course not! Saying "OK" is an option, not a requirement. Sometimes, you want to go with the flow to make your relationships run smoothly; sometimes you need to speak up in a calm and respectful way. In Raj's case, if he doesn't want the popcorn, he could just say, "No, thanks."

AVOID TINY-BIT-EMPTY THINKING

You've probably heard about how some people see a glass as half empty and some people see a glass as half full. In other words, looking at what's happening around them, some people notice what's wrong, and some people notice what's right. Both views are true, but the people who notice only what's wrong are overlooking the positives. That could make them feel discouraged, upset, or overwhelmed. They might be cutting themselves off from enjoying what's right.

It may seem like the people who notice only the positive are better off, but they could be overlooking real problems. If they paid attention to those problems, maybe they could take action to solve them.

The wisest people are usually the ones who see the whole glass, both empty and full, because they can see what's right and can also address or at least understand what's wrong. Seeing the good along with the bad can also make the good seem sweeter.

There's a fourth group of people: These people look at a glass that's almost completely full and focus on a tiny drop that spilled.

Tiny-Bit-Empty Thinking means getting stuck focusing on the tiniest thing that is not exactly how you want. This kind of thinking makes people very unhappy. It's not smart to have your happiness depend on everything being perfect. Can you guess why that's not a good idea? It's because *almost always* things are not exactly perfect! That's just life. Everything and everyone is imperfect (including you!). So if you decide, "I can only be happy if everything is perfect!" you're signing up for a lot of unhappiness.

Seeing more than just what's not perfect helps you feel happier. Raj had some annoying things happen today, but if he thinks about it, he can probably remember a lot of good or at least OK things that also happened today.

PRACTICE BEING FLEXIBLE

Try this experiment: Grab the edge of a table. Try to bend it. Nope. No matter how hard you try, it doesn't bend. Things that don't bend are called *rigid*.

People can have rigid responses when they refuse to bend in their thinking or actions.

Rigid: Can't Bend

Can you guess what the problems are with rigid responses?

Rigid responses leave people stuck when life doesn't happen exactly the way they want it to happen. It's also not fun to be around someone who is responding in rigid ways because they argue a lot and won't cooperate.

Now let's try another experiment: Grab a rubber band. Try to bend it. Yup, that works. It completely bends, twists, and even stretches any way you try, without much effort.

The opposite of rigid is **flexible**, which means that something—or someone—can bend.

Flexible: Can Bend

Flexible responses are about being able to go with the flow and adjust to unexpected events or consider what other people want or need. Often they involve **compromise**, which means doing partly what you want and partly what the other

> Flexible responses help you move forward when things aren't perfect.

person wants. Flexible responses help you move forward when things aren't perfect, and they can help a friendship grow and last because they show you care about more than what you want.

FIGURE OUT WHEN AND HOW TO TALK ABOUT WHAT'S WRONG

How we talk about our feelings can have a big effect on friendships. We need to tell friends about our feelings to build closeness and get help or comfort. On the other hand, if most of what we say is negative, or if we say it in mean ways, that's not fun to be around.

Here are some tips for talking about grumpy feelings with friends:

1. Pick the right person, time, and place. Choose someone who is likely to listen and respond warmly. Choose a time when that person isn't super busy or distracted. Talking about feelings in private is usually better than in public. Also, some problems are better to talk about with adults than with other kids, because the adults are better able to handle them.

2. Talk to friends in a way that makes it easy for them to listen. If you yell, it's harder for other people to hear you. (Can you explain why making your point at a loud volume makes it less likely people will listen?) Yelling at people will make them want to yell back or move far away from you.

3. Ask for what you want or need. Friends can't know what you want from them unless you tell them. Before talking to friends about your feelings, it's often useful to figure out how you want them to respond. Do you want them to help you solve a problem, distract you, or just listen? If you tell a friend what you want, you're more likely to get that response. You could ask, "Could you please___?" or "Would you mind___?" You could also say, "It would help if you/we could___."

Here are two kids who feel grumpy and are telling a friend about what's bothering them. Which kid is more likely to get a good response from their friend? What do you think each kid is doing right or wrong?

I'm in a very grumpy mood right now. My Spanish teacher assigned a big project and my shoes are squeezing my toes. Would you mind walking with me to the library? It would help me feel better to have some company.

Well, the first kid is definitely not doing a good job of communicating with his friend! He's taking his mood out on the friend. How do you think his friend is likely to respond? Not well. That friend will probably defend his shoes and how he says hi. The friend might also accuse the first kid of being mean, or say, "What's your problem?!" and walk away.

The second kid does a much better job of communicating. Notice what that kid is doing:

*   Labeling his feeling (grumpy)

*   Recognizing that this feeling is right now, not forever

*   Explaining why he's feeling that way, rather than blaming the friend

*   Asking for the response he wants from his friend

Wow! That's powerful communication! The friend is very likely to respond in a caring way.

ADDRESS THE UNDERLYING CAUSES OF GRUMPINESS

Sometimes feeling grumpy leads to **Emotional Spillover**. That happens when feelings about one situation affect how you respond in a later situation. For example, if you're feeling upset about how you did on a spelling test, but then you yell at a friend for asking to borrow a piece of paper, that's Emotional Spillover onto the friend. Yelling at a friend won't help you learn the spelling words or do better on the next test, and it's hurtful to your friend.

Sometimes kids think, *Well, I'm grumpy! So I should be able to yell at everyone!* That's not a good idea. It's definitely not kind, and it won't help fix whatever is causing your grumpiness. If you're feeling grumpy, try not to take your mood out on other people. Instead, try to figure out what might help.

If you notice that you're often grumpy, you may want to think about some of the things that can lead to grumpiness. For example, sometimes you may feel grumpy and less able to handle frustrating situations when you're tired or hungry or haven't gotten enough exercise. Luckily these problems are easy to fix!

Talk with your grown-up about changes to your schedule that might help, like having a snack at a certain time, or getting more exercise, or maybe turning out the lights a bit earlier. Most kids don't want to go to bed earlier. But if you find that you're often grumpy—and especially if it's affecting your friendships or other relationships—it may be worth trying an experiment to see if that helps your mood. You could try going to sleep a little earlier or getting up a little later or making some other changes to help you stay asleep (no one likes being woken up in the night).

10

The Opposites of Anger Are Acceptance, Compassion, and Bigger-Than-Me Happiness

Anger gives us clues about what matters to us. We feel angry with friends when we think they're treating us unfairly or doing something that blocks us from what we want. Anger makes us want to take action against something. It can give us energy to speak up or to solve problems.

But sometimes kids act on their anger in ways that hurt friends or other people. That's not kind. It also usually ends up creating more problems for the angry kid.

Sometimes when we're feeling very angry, we need to give ourselves space to cool down so we can think clearly. We don't want to do or say something we'll regret. Each of the kids in this section either did or thought about doing something unkind. Bao threw his friend's controller, Miriam wanted to prevent Anika from being friends with Eva, Lola said mean things about Penelope, and Raj insulted his friend's snack. All of these actions could hurt their friendships and make them feel even more mad.

Talking with friends is one way to deal with angry feelings. For instance, Bao could apologize. He could also talk with his friend about playing a different game. Miriam could talk about how much she enjoys Anika's

119

company to strengthen their friendship. Raj could tell his friend about his difficult day to get some support.

Often the best way to deal with angry feelings is to think about the situation differently. If we change how we think, we can change how we feel.

Thinking differently could help the kids in this section feel less angry. Bao could remind himself that Jeffrey probably didn't mean to break his building and that a friendship is more important than a game. Miriam could accept that Anika is allowed to have other friends. Lola could let go of her Enemy Thinking by realizing she wants to be a kind person, even if Penelope isn't.

Beyond thoughts and actions, another way to deal with anger about friends is by looking for the Opposite Feelings. Anger is focused on caring about what you want. The opposite of anger isn't telling yourself, "I don't care." It's actually caring *more* for both yourself *and* others.

Acceptance and compassion are two feelings that are the opposite of anger. **Acceptance** means liking people the way they are. **Compassion** is a feeling that comes when we look at people with kind eyes. We have compassion for others when we see things from their point of view, instead of just criticizing or blaming them for what we don't like.

It's often easier to be angry. But it's more rewarding to be compassionate, and it's a kind thing to do because your focus is on others and not just on yourself.

> If we change how we think, we can change how we feel.

120

Acceptance

Compassion

Compassion for other people can be helpful for easing anger about friends, but sometimes we also need to have compassion for ourselves.

Compassion for Ourselves

122

Acceptance and compassion can melt away anger at others and even at ourselves. It's about having a generous heart and seeing the best in people.

Another feeling that's the opposite of anger is *Bigger-Than-Me Happiness*. This feeling happens when we choose to do the right thing, especially when it's difficult to do that. When we act in ways that make the world a better place, we feel good. We feel connected to others. We gain a sense of peace that quiets anger.

Bigger-Than-Me Happiness isn't the same as "Yeah! It's my birthday!" happiness. It's quieter and gentler but also wider and deeper. You may have had this feeling when you've forgiven a friend or done something kind for someone for no reason at all.

Acceptance, compassion, and Bigger-Than-Me Happiness can help ease anger by helping you care about more than just what you want.

Bigger-Than-Me Happiness

When you're feeling angry, notice that, but don't just act on it without thinking. Try to **See the Bigger Picture**. That means looking beyond what you want by considering what others think, feel, want, or need. It also means seeing beyond the present moment by thinking about what came before and what's likely to happen next. You don't have to erase your anger. Feelings are never dangerous, and your anger is giving you information. The question is, what are you going to do with it? Focusing on the Opposite Feelings will soften your anger and help you figure out the right way forward. Maybe you'll speak up. Maybe you'll let it go. Maybe you'll change how you do things. Maybe you'll balance out your anger with Opposite Feelings and move toward Bigger-Than-Me Happiness.

THINK ABOUT IT!

Learning to manage anger about friends is difficult. It takes a lot of practice. Here are some questions to help you think through how you've dealt with anger in the past and how you want to deal with it moving forward.

* Can you think of a time when you felt furious at a friend? What did the friend do? How did you handle it? What would your friend say happened? If you could have a do-over, would you change anything about how you dealt with things?

* What do you do to keep your Friendship Bag of Marbles full?

* Have you ever felt jealous of a friend's other friend? How did you handle that?

* Have you ever known a kid who you thought of as your enemy? What led to that? Why do you think it's important to let go of Enemy Thinking?

* Avoiding taking your grumpy mood out on other people can be difficult. What might help you if you're feeling grumpy?

* Do you think you're more often rigid or flexible with friends? What is one time when you chose to be flexible even though things weren't perfect?

PART III
Feeling Sad about Friends

I howl at the moon when I feel sad. By day, dogs are playful, but by night we are in touch with the profound loneliness of life.

That would be a you thing. The only time I feel sad is when my humans run out of cat treats.

Sadness is the emotion we feel when we're missing something or someone. Feeling *sad* hurts like an ache in the heart.

Sadness with friends is about wanting something we don't have. It can happen when we lose a friend or when things don't turn out the way we wanted. Sometimes we feel sad when we believe something is missing in our friendships.

Even though it's painful, sadness—like every other emotion—is useful. It helps us figure out what matters to us. It can lead us to seek comfort, which brings us closer to others. It can also inspire us to make changes to try to fill in what's missing.

Here are some ideas for dealing with feeling sad about friends.

11
Feeling Grief

SIMON'S CHALLENGE: MISSING A FARAWAY FRIEND

Simon is very sad because his friend moved away. This was a big loss for him, so of course he's *grieving*. *Grief* means that aching feeling from knowing something or someone you cared deeply about is no longer with you. Miguel was a good friend, so it makes sense that Simon is grieving now that Miguel is far away.

It may be possible for Simon and Miguel to stay in touch by video chat or messaging, or playing games together online. Maybe they could even visit each other someday. Doing what you can to stay connected to a friend who has moved away can make you both feel better about being apart. But your relationship definitely won't be the same as it was.

FEELINGS STORY: SIMON'S RESPONSE TO MIGUEL MOVING AWAY

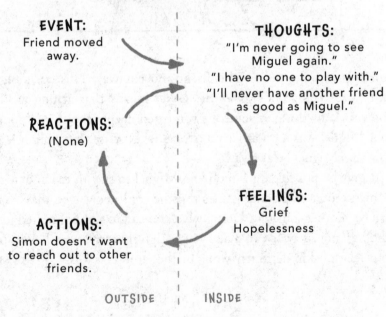

EVENT:
Friend moved away.

THOUGHTS:
"I'm never going to see Miguel again."
"I have no one to play with."
"I'll never have another friend as good as Miguel."

REACTIONS:
(None)

FEELINGS:
Grief
Hopelessness

ACTIONS:
Simon doesn't want to reach out to other friends.

OUTSIDE   INSIDE

130

Looking at Simon's Feelings Story, the starting event is Miguel moving away. The thoughts Simon tells himself about this focus on predicting lots of bad things: never seeing Miguel and never having another close friend. This leads him to feel grief over the loss but also hopelessness about the future. ***Hopelessness*** means feeling down because we have no hope that the future will be better.

Because he's feeling ***hopeless***, Simon doesn't want to reach out to other friends. That's understandable, but it also keeps him feeling sad, and it doesn't bring Miguel back. Because Simon stays away from other friends, he doesn't get the comfort or fun that could help him feel a little less sad.

Have you ever lost a friend? Friendships can end because someone moves. They can also end after an argument or when kids drift apart because they develop different interests and don't spend much time together. Let's look at some things you can do when you're grieving over a lost friendship.

ACCEPT YOUR FEELINGS

When we can't change a situation, we can be kind to ourselves by noticing and accepting our feelings. Simon can't control the fact that Miguel had to move, but he can be kind to himself by recognizing, "This hurts. I'm sad. I miss Miguel."

Sometimes people judge their feelings. They think, "I shouldn't feel this way!" or "It's babyish to feel this way!" But you feel what you feel, and that's OK. Feelings aren't good or bad; they're just information.

Telling someone who cares about you how you're feeling is a good idea. When you share your feelings, it's like letting someone else carry half the weight of those feelings. Simon's mom can't bring Miguel back, but she can offer comfort and understanding. That feels good.

> When we can't change a situation, we can be kind to ourselves by noticing and accepting our feelings.

You may also want to do something to express your feelings in a way that puts them into solid form. You could write about fun times you had with your friend or create a collage with pictures you draw or photos of you and the friend. This helps you hold on to your memories. It also gives you a way to show how you're feeling now. You may decide to share what you create with your faraway friend or with your grown-up.

DO THINGS TO HELP YOURSELF FEEL A LITTLE BIT BETTER

It's often useful to ask yourself, "How would I treat a friend who is in my situation?"

132

In Simon's case, he definitely wouldn't tell a grieving friend, "Snap out of it!" or "You shouldn't feel that way!" That's not realistic, and it's not kind. Instead, Simon would probably try to be extra nice to the friend, even offer comfort or a distraction.

So how could Simon be extra nice to *himself*? The same way: find comfort or fun distractions.

Here are some things that might help him feel a little bit better:

* Listen to music

* Watch a funny show or read a funny book

* Go for a bike ride

* Spend time with a pet

* Build or make something creative

* Hang out with other friends

* Go for a walk with family members

* Bake cookies with a grown-up

* Learn something new

* Play a game

* Decorate his room

* Bundle himself in a cozy blanket

What do you do when you want to comfort yourself?

BE OPEN TO OTHER RELATIONSHIPS

Simon is absolutely right: no one can replace Miguel. But that doesn't mean he can't build other friendships.

Sometimes kids think they can't make new friends because it would be disloyal to their old friends. This is not true. In fact, because Miguel cares about Simon, he would definitely want Simon to find new friends rather than stay lonely.

To find possible friends, Simon can think about who seems kind and who likes to do the same things he does. He may want to try joining new clubs or activities. He should definitely try talking and playing with kids he sees at school or in his neighborhood.

New friendships aren't as easy or comfortable as old friendships. It takes time to get close to someone. The sooner Simon starts spending time with other kids he likes, the sooner he can build new close friendships. The new friendships won't replace Miguel. They don't have to. They can be fun and meaningful on their own.

GIVE IT TIME

When you're dealing with a big loss, it seems like you'll always be sad. Because they were so close, Simon will probably miss Miguel for a long time. But that grief doesn't have to close him off to happiness. He can miss Miguel *and* enjoy his life.

Sometimes a wave of sadness hits. Maybe you see or do something that reminds you of your old friend or maybe you have a problem and wish your friend were there to talk to. A wave of sadness can be very painful, but it won't always stay at an intense level. You may cry when you're feeling very sad. That's OK. In fact, sometimes we feel better after a good cry, kind of like we're releasing the heavy feelings we've been carrying. Crying also signals to others that we're hurting and need comfort. Just ride that wave of sadness when it hits by noticing the feelings and waiting for them to pass.

Whatever you're feeling now is about right now. You won't always feel this way. One of the amazing things about feelings is that they soften over time.

12
Feeling Disappointed

DIVYA'S CHALLENGE: NOT MAKING THE TEAM

Divya is very **disappointed** about not making it onto the A-team. **Disappointment** is the feeling when we don't get something we want and expected to get. Divya really thought she'd be on the more advanced team with her friends. Seeing her friends happy and excited while she's left behind makes her disappointment worse.

This is tough. Anyone would be upset about being left out like this.

FEELINGS STORY: DIVYA'S RESPONSE TO BEING PICKED FOR THE B-TEAM

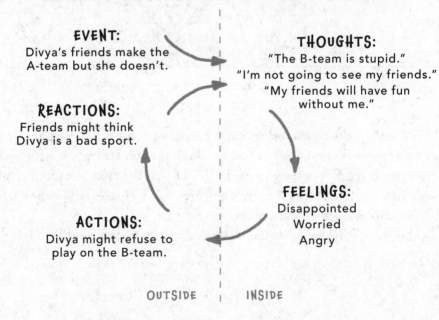

EVENT:
Divya's friends make the A-team but she doesn't.

THOUGHTS:
"The B-team is stupid."
"I'm not going to see my friends."
"My friends will have fun without me."

REACTIONS:
Friends might think Divya is a bad sport.

FEELINGS:
Disappointed
Worried
Angry

ACTIONS:
Divya might refuse to play on the B-team.

OUTSIDE | INSIDE

138

Let's take a look at Divya's Feelings Story: The event that starts the story is Divya not making the A-team when her friends do. She immediately has thoughts that the B-team is stupid. She also imagines her friends having fun without her.

These thoughts make her feel disappointed and worried. Divya is surprised—and not in a good way—to be put on the B-team. She may also feel angry at the coach.

In terms of actions, Divya is considering not playing on the B-team. A part of Divya probably wants to sulk and refuse to try. But another part of her probably knows that that's not a good idea. No matter how much she wants or even thinks she deserves to be on the A-team, it's the coach's decision, so she needs to accept it. Also, how might people react if she sulks? Her friends might think she's a bad sport. It would also get in the way of her making friends and having fun on the B-team.

Divya has two challenges to deal with:

* How can she manage her feelings of disappointment?

* How can she stay connected with her friends when she's spending a lot of time apart from them?

Let's take a look at some ideas that might help if you're in a situation like Divya's and need to move past disappointment.

TRUST IN YOUR STRENGTH

If you have a big disappointment, it's important to notice your feelings. Letting go of the future you imagined is a loss. Of course, you feel sad to realize it's not going to happen (at least not right now)!

But here's the good news: you're strong enough to handle disappointment.

Ugh. Maybe that doesn't sound like good news, but it really is. It means that although disappointment is painful, the pain doesn't last forever.

You may want to ask yourself, "How long will this matter?"

Have you ever fallen and scraped your knee? That really hurts! In the moment, you might even cry. But then what happens? You clean the cut, you get a bandage, and little by little, the scrape heals, and soon you are not even bothered by it.

> You are strong enough to handle disappointment.

Disappointment works the same way. The worst moment is when it first happens. But then, as time passes, you start to get used to it, and it doesn't matter as much anymore.

In Divya's case, the moment she learns that she will be on the B-team is the worst. A week later, she'll probably still wish she were on the A-team with her friends, but maybe she'll also be having fun with the other kids on the B-team.

A month later, when she's competing in games with her teammates, she'll probably still have some twinges of disappointment that she's not with her other friends, but she'll also enjoy the excitement of the games, cheering on her teammates, and going out for pizza after the games to celebrate the B-team's efforts.

How about next year? Will Divya still be feeling disappointed about not making the A-team? If she does, it will be a fleeting moment. But she will have had so many other experiences by then that this event will be a distant memory.

Sometimes kids say, "I'll be happy when . . ." or even "I can only be happy if . . ." This is a misunderstanding of happiness. We can't make our happiness depend on everything around us being exactly the way we want, because that never happens. And that's OK. You're strong enough to find happiness in lots of different situations.

Notice that the "cure" for Divya's disappointment isn't changing things so she gets what she wants. She's not going to get the coach to put her on the A-team at this point. Her world isn't going to change, but her feelings will. The disappointment will fade in importance. She's strong enough to move on. She even has the opportunity to make the best of the situation by being friendly, cooperative, and enthusiastic. She can have fun playing a sport she enjoys even though she's not on the top team.

If she works hard and practices on the B-team, her soccer-playing skills will definitely improve. They might even improve enough for her to make the A-team next year.

One of the wonderful things about life is we just don't know what's around the corner: a new friendship, a new interest, a fun experience . . . To discover these possibilities and write the next chapter of her life, Divya needs to acknowledge her disappointment first and then let it go and focus on what's next.

Keep Going!
You Don't Know What's around the Corner

PLAY THE WELL-AT-LEAST GAME

Sometimes adults tell kids who are feeling disappointed, "Look on the bright side!" That often feels hard to do. When you're very disappointed, you don't *want* to find the good in a bad situation. But you might be able to find things that are not so bad or even things that could be worse!

The **Well-at-Least Game** involves imagining a worse situation than the one you're facing so the actual disappointment doesn't seem so bad. Divya might tell herself something like this:

* "*Well, at least* I get to play on a soccer team, and I might make new friends there."

* "*Well, at least* I'll still see my friends at recess and lunch and if we get together on the weekends. I could even watch some of their games."

* "*Well, at least* I'll get to start and have more playing time in B-team games than I would in A-team games."

* "*Well, at least* I can try out for the A-team again next year."

You can play the Well-at-Least Game in lots of different situations and even imagine silly comparisons. For instance, here's what you could tell yourself if you're disappointed because a friend got sick with a cold and canceled a hangout:

* "*Well, at least* my friend didn't come over and puke on my bed."

* "*Well, at least* my friend didn't move to Antarctica."

* "*Well, at least* my friend wasn't eaten by a Tyrannosaurus Rex."

By comparison, a canceled playdate due to a cold doesn't seem so bad!

EXPRESS SUPPORT FOR YOUR FRIENDS

In order to stay connected with her friends, Divya needs to be supportive of them, even though she's disappointed for herself. This is very, very difficult, but it is what good friends do.

You can have more than one feeling at the same time: you can be sad for yourself *and* happy for your friends. Out of caring for your friends, you don't want to do things that will spoil their happiness, because that's not kind. Finding a way to be happy for your friends is not being fake; it's being generous.

In this situation, to be a good friend, Divya needs to tell her friends, "Congratulations!" and really mean it.

> Finding a way to be happy for your friends is generous.

If she wants to stay connected with her friends, she needs to show interest in what they're doing over time too. In a couple of weeks, she could ask them about their team and how their games went. She should also tell them about her team in a positive way. She might even want to go watch some of their games so she can cheer them on. That would be a very caring thing to do. Her friends might also support her by coming to watch Divya and her teammates play.

Because they won't see each other at practice, Divya can also make an extra effort to get together with her friends and to have fun with them at other times. That shows her friends they matter to her. And when soccer season ends, she'll still have those connections with her friends.

143

13

Feeling Ashamed and Envious

ZACK'S CHALLENGE:
BELIEVING HE'S NOT GOOD ENOUGH

Zack is feeling very sad. He's also having two other very painful emotions: shame and envy. **Shame** is how we feel when we believe our whole self is wrong or not good enough. **Envy** is the feeling when we compare ourselves to others and wish we could be as good as them.

How do you feel reading this story about Zack? Maybe you've sometimes felt the way he does. Maybe he reminds you of someone you know. Maybe you feel sorry for Zack. Maybe you're responding like the cat and dog and want to comfort him.

FEELINGS STORY: ZACK'S RESPONSE TO TRIPPING AND DROPPING HIS BOOKS

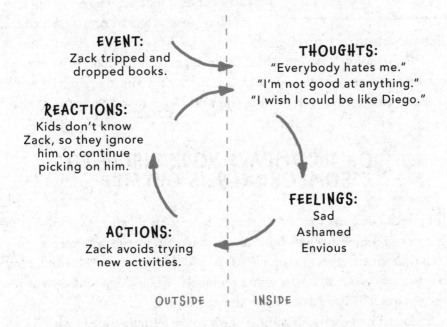

EVENT:
Zack tripped and dropped books.

THOUGHTS:
"Everybody hates me."
"I'm not good at anything."
"I wish I could be like Diego."

REACTIONS:
Kids don't know Zack, so they ignore him or continue picking on him.

FEELINGS:
Sad
Ashamed
Envious

ACTIONS:
Zack avoids trying new activities.

OUTSIDE | INSIDE

Let's think about Zack's Feelings Story to understand what's going on.

The event that got things rolling happened a while ago: it was when he dropped his books and the other kids began making fun of him. This led him to think all kinds of mean things about himself: He believes he's not good at anything and no one likes him. Comparing himself to the popular Diego makes Zack even more aware of what he sees as his flaws. It's like he's grading himself and giving himself an F on everything.

These thoughts lead to his painful feelings of sadness, shame, and envy. Then what does he do? Looking at action, he decides to avoid going to the robotics club. He also probably stays away from the other kids as much as he can at school. This guarantees that he's not going to make friends, and it makes it more likely that the unkind kids will continue teasing him because he doesn't have the support of friends around him. His Feelings Story leaves him very stuck.

> Stop grading yourself!

So how does Zack get unstuck? It's not easy, but it is doable. He needs to stop avoiding new activities and new people. But to do that, Zack first needs to change the way he thinks about himself.

If you've ever felt ashamed like Zack, you may think that the way to feel better is to eliminate all your flaws or differences. But that's not possible. The real answer is to stop grading yourself! Here are some ways to do that.

DON'T COMPARE YOUR INSIDE TO SOMEONE ELSE'S OUTSIDE

It's easy to imagine that other people have it all together. Zack looks at Diego and sees someone who everyone looks up to and who seems to do well with no effort and no problems. Wouldn't that be nice?! It would, but it's probably not real. *Everyone* has problems. We just don't necessarily see them, especially if we don't know the person well.

It doesn't make sense to compare how you're feeling inside to what someone else looks like on the outside, in public. Maybe they don't have exactly the same problems you do, but they're human, so they definitely have struggles. You just don't know what they might be dealing with.

148

TREAT YOURSELF THE WAY YOU WOULD A FRIEND

Zack is hanging on to the memory of tripping and is beating himself up about it. Do you think he would respond the same way to a friend who had tripped? Probably not.

When you make a mistake, try to speak to yourself the same way you would to a friend—with kindness. For instance, if a friend tripped and dropped all their books, what would you say? You definitely wouldn't say the things that Zack is saying to himself. Saying, "You're so stupid! You can't do anything right!" would be a very mean thing to say to anyone.

Instead, you'd probably try to comfort the friend and help them not feel bad about tripping. You might say something like "Are you OK? Let me help you pick those books up. It's easy to trip here. It could happen to anyone."

Then you'd move on. You and your friend have more interesting things to talk and think about than going over and over past mistakes.

Try to treat yourself with the same kindness you would show to a friend.

When I want to be kind to myself, it usually involves tuna casserole. It's like the old saying, "Time and tuna casserole heal all wounds."

I haven't heard that saying before, but I like it!

FIGURE OUT WHAT DIFFERENCES MEAN TO YOU

Everyone is unique. Sometimes kids are proud of their differences, but sometimes being different from other people around you can lead you to feel disconnected and somehow not good enough. It's especially hard when differences make you the target of teasing or bullying.

There are so many ways that kids can feel different! Having diabetes or ADHD, wearing glasses or braces, being the tallest or shortest kid in class, and even being in a lower or higher math group are all differences that might make you feel down about yourself. Even being raised by grandparents, or being a different race or religion, or speaking a different language can make kids feel different and separate from the kids around them.

You can't control what other people think of your differences, but it's important to figure out what those differences mean to you. That's part of understanding who you are as a person. This is not something you're going to decide once and for all. Your sense of self is likely to change as you get older and when you're with different people or in different situations. Here are some things to think about as you're learning to better understand yourself.

Question the "shoulds." The first thing to do is to question any beliefs or messages you've heard about how you should be. For instance, who decides what you should look like or what you should be good at? The world would be a very boring place if everyone were exactly the same!

Look for the positive side of differences. You may want to ask yourself whether there are good things that go along with your differences. Maybe you have trouble paying attention, but you're very creative. Maybe your differences make you similar to people you love, like your family and friends. There also might be famous people who have your differences and have made wonderful contributions to the world. Maybe your differences connect you to a certain group or culture with rich history and traditions. You may become proud of your differences if you learn more about them.

See the whole picture. It's also important to see your differences as part—not all—of who you are. Have you ever zoomed in very close on a picture on a computer, to the point where it just looks like a bunch of colored blobs? Focusing in on one blob doesn't tell you a thing about what the picture is. You need to zoom out to see the whole big picture.

The same is true with you. Focusing on just one part of yourself doesn't make sense. It's the whole picture of you that matters.

PLAN HOW YOU WANT TO RESPOND

In some situations, you may need to be ready to handle questions or comments about your differences—whether they are meant to be rude or not. How you respond will depend on the situation and your relationship with the person making the comment. Talk with your grown-up to figure out how you might respond to rude comments. Here are a bunch of possibilities:

* **Give a short explanation.** Sometimes people aren't trying to be mean when they comment on a difference. They're just curious. You don't necessarily have to answer their questions, but you might decide to give a short explanation. For instance, you could say, "Those are my hearing aids. They help me hear better."

* **Brush it off.** If you don't want to deal with discussing the difference at that time or with that person, you might want to shrug or say, "Hmmm," and change the subject.

* **Stand up for yourself.** Sometimes people do things that make you feel uncomfortable. They may not realize it unless you say something, and if you don't tell them it bothers you, they might

keep doing it! Start with the word "I" so you emphasize what you want. This works better than starting with the word "you," which could make the other person likely to argue or defend what they did or said. For example, you could say, "I don't like it when people touch my hair. Please don't."

* **Call them on it.** If someone is being mean to you, you may want to speak up clearly and firmly about what they're doing wrong. For example, you could say, "It's not OK to say that" or "That's a rude question." Then walk away.

* **Talk to an adult in charge.** If the comments are very hurtful, or they keep happening, you may need to tell an adult about the situation. If the first adult you talk to doesn't help, talk to a different adult. You have the right to be treated with respect. Sometimes an adult has to step in to make sure that happens.

My difference is that I have exceptionally long and lovely whiskers. When people comment on them, I invite them to join my fan club!

Does that happen often?

Not as often as I'd like!

FIND YOUR PEOPLE

Feeling different in one group doesn't mean you'll feel different in every group. Sometimes you just have to look for the right group. Finding your people means looking for those who share your interests, perspective, or background. It feels good to be able to walk in and think, "Here are kids like me."

You may have to be creative about looking for your group. Think about what matters to you and what you like to do. Be open to new activities, especially if someone who knows you and loves you suggests them. Zack's mom suggested that he try going to the robotics club. Maybe he'll like it and maybe he won't, but it's worth exploring. Maybe he'll find his people in the robotics club. Or maybe he'll just get a better understanding of where else he could look. Listening to a grown-up who loves you can sometimes be a good bet!

NEVER PUT YOURSELF DOWN IN PUBLIC

Sometimes kids think they have to announce to the world their flaws and failings. They'll say things like "I'm so stupid. I'm such a loser. I can't do anything right." Maybe they're looking for attention, or maybe they think they need to put themselves down before anyone else does.

How do you think other people feel if they hear you put yourself down? The first time it happens, other people might respond by trying to reassure you, "Oh, you're not a loser!"

But if you keep insisting strongly, "Yes, I am a total loser!" eventually, they're likely to feel annoyed.

Listening to anyone put themselves down gets old fast. It's really not much fun to argue with someone about whether or not they're a loser. Also, if you keep insisting that you're a loser, you might convince people that you are. But you aren't. Nobody is a total loser, so change the subject. Focus instead on playing together or talking about more interesting topics.

FOCUS ON WHAT YOU CAN GIVE

Zack is feeling *envious* because he believes Diego is better than him—more popular, more accomplished. This comparison is not helpful. There will always be people in the world who are better/faster/smarter than you are. So what?

Imagine the world's greatest basketball player. (Maybe you have an opinion about who that is!) Now, think of the other players on that person's team. Should the second-best player give up and go home? Why not? All the other players on the team aren't as good as the world's greatest player. Maybe they should all go home!

No, they shouldn't. Even though they're not as good as the world's greatest player—and probably never will be—the other players have something to give to the team. The game wouldn't be much fun if it was just the greatest player standing on the court alone.

So, if you're not the best at something, that's OK. You can always work on improving from where you are now with learning and practice—and that's a good thing. It means you'll have more to give. But don't decide you can only like yourself if you're the best. Almost no one is. Even people who are the best at one thing are not the best at everything.

We are each unique. That means you have something only you can give to the world. What you give doesn't have to be amazing. You can give just by adding a little bit of kindness to the world. Here are some possible kind actions you could take:

* Make a special birthday card for a friend.

* Explain the homework to a classmate.

* Work hard on a home project.

* Pick up some litter in the park.

* Play with a younger child.

* Greet a neighbor.

* Plant some flowers.

* Ask your grown-up, "How was your day?" and really listen to the answer.

* Help make dinner.

Figuring out what you can give to others—and doing it—matters much more than being "the best."

REMEMBER: TRUE FRIENDS ACCEPT YOU AS YOU ARE

Think of someone you love—maybe a family member. Would you love that person more if they were smarter, taller, richer, more famous, or better looking? Of course not! You care about them because they are who they are.

Isn't it possible that the people who love you feel the same way? They love you exactly as you are. That's it. *Love doesn't have to be earned.*

It works the same way with good friends. They like you for who you are, not for who you think you ought to be. You are enough. Trying to be perfect won't help you make more friends or become closer to the ones you have, but being kind and doing fun things together will.

you are enough.

155

14
Feeling Lonely

**KIKO'S CHALLENGE:
LONGING FOR A CLOSE FRIEND**

Poor Kiko! She's having an experience that most people have had at some point: feeling alone or *lonely* in a crowd. She is surrounded by other kids but doesn't feel connected to them. It sounds like she has friends, but she doesn't have the kind of special, close friendship that she wants. Even though there are plenty of people around she could play with, seeing other kids who seem to have a special friendship makes her feel like an outsider. *Loneliness* means feeling sad and disconnected from others.

FEELINGS STORY: KIKO'S RESPONSE TO BEING ALONE ON THE PLAYGROUND

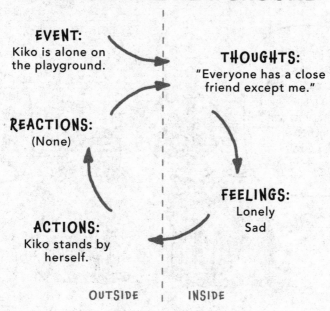

EVENT:
Kiko is alone on the playground.

THOUGHTS:
"Everyone has a close friend except me."

REACTIONS:
(None)

FEELINGS:
Lonely
Sad

ACTIONS:
Kiko stands by herself.

OUTSIDE | INSIDE

Let's take a look at Kiko's Feelings Story. The event that sets things in motion is being alone on the playground. Sometimes people can feel perfectly happy when they're alone, but that's not what's happening with Kiko. The thought that runs through her head is "Everyone has a close friend except me." Is this true? Probably not. Some kids have a close friend, but not everyone at every moment.

Her thoughts make her feel sad and lonely. Even though other kids are nearby, Kiko sees herself as separate, different, and unwanted. Ouch.

So what does she do in response to those feelings? Nothing. She continues to stand by herself.

And the reaction she gets from others? Also nothing. The other kids don't even know she wants to be closer to them, so they're not responding.

To change her Feelings Story, Kiko is going to have to find some ways to think and do things differently. Here are some ideas of what you can do when you're feeling lonely.

FOCUS ON TWO POWERFUL WORDS

When you're feeling down, it's easy to believe that what is now will always be. But that's often not true. Adding two powerful words to your thoughts can remind you of this. The words are: *right now*.

In Kiko's case, she could tell herself, "I don't have any close friends *right now*." Can you hear the power of those words? They don't cancel out whatever thoughts came before, but they lessen their impact by making room for other possibilities.

> Whatever your situation is, it probably won't last forever.

Adding the words *right now* is a good way to remind yourself that whatever your situation is, it probably won't last forever. This can help you move forward and think about what to do next.

160

TAKE A SMALL STEP TOWARD WHERE YOU WANT TO BE

It takes time to build close friendships. If you're feeling sad about not having close friends, you probably can't solve that overnight. But it might help to ask yourself, "What's one step I can take today or tomorrow toward building closer friendships?"

Here are some possibilities:

* Look around for kids who are having fun at recess. Join that group by watching what they're doing and then sliding into the action without interrupting.

* Think of who seems nice in your class or after-school activities. Be sure to say hi to them and try to chat with them. Maybe give them a sincere compliment or do a small kindness for them. All of these show you're open to friendship.

* Get involved in a new activity where you could meet people who like to do things you like to do.

* Consider reaching out to an old friend. Sometimes friendships end with a big blowup. Sometimes they just fade away because kids aren't able to spend time together, or they're interested in different things. Either way, if the friendship was good before, it might be worth trying to build it up again now.

* Invite someone to come over or plan a fun activity together. Spending fun time with just one other person is the single best thing you can do to deepen your friendship. You don't have to be close to someone to get together; getting together helps you become closer.

* Be patient and keep trying. It takes time and effort to deepen a friendship.

BE OPEN TO ALL KINDS OF FRIENDSHIPS

Lots of kids wish for a very best friend. When that happens, if the best friend is kind and caring, it can be wonderful. But you can enjoy all kinds of friendships. You can enjoy a neighborhood friend, a soccer friend, a math class friend, and even a cousin friend. Each of these people can add fun and connection to your life. Maybe, over time, they'll deepen into closer friendships, or maybe they'll stay just as they are. Don't let the current lack of a best friend get in the way of enjoying these other friendships.

LET SOMEONE SEE THE REAL YOU

Most of us want to look good around other people, so we tend to hide the less-than-perfect parts of ourselves. But perfection is cold and not much fun to be around. When we act like we're perfect, we're *acting*, instead of being real. Trying to look perfect gets in the way of true friendships. It's also exhausting.

On the other hand, when we're more honest about our feelings, struggles, and challenges, we create the possibility for real connection. Sharing those less-than-perfect parts of ourselves lets friends get close to us.

This doesn't mean that you should tell everything to everybody. Not everyone is kind, and not everyone wants or needs to know all personal parts of your life. But choosing to confide in someone you like and who likes you back can be a powerful way to deepen a friendship.

Sharing the less-than-perfect, personal side of you tells that person, "I trust you." That's a gift. It lets that person get to know you at a deeper level. Also, when you share the personal side of yourself, your friend might do the same. That's how close friendships grow.

If you decide to confide in someone, pace yourself. You don't want to overwhelm your friend by confiding too much too fast. You also don't want all or most of your conversations to be about difficult topics. That's not fun. Plus, you need to give your friend a chance to confide in you too, to keep your friendship balanced.

So what kinds of things could you share? Here are some ideas:

* Something you worry about

* A time when you made a mistake

* Something you're struggling with

* A time when you felt hurt

* Something you regret doing

* A time when you felt sad

* Something you hope for but don't know if it will happen

All of these topics are about vulnerability. **_Vulnerability_** means letting someone know you well enough that you could get hurt. That's a risk. If someone makes fun of you or blabs your secrets after you confide in them, that would hurt a lot. It takes courage to let yourself be **_vulnerable_** with a friend. But taking that risk is the only way to build real closeness. A good friend will respond to your sharing personal topics with comfort and maybe even "Me too!" That feels good.

BE A GOOD FRIEND TO YOURSELF

Friends matter. They make the good times more fun and the hard times easier. But no matter what is or isn't happening with friends, it's important for you to be a good friend to yourself. What do you think that means?

> Treat
> yourself with
> kindness.

Mostly, it means you need to treat yourself with kindness. So, don't say mean things about yourself. Do take care of yourself. Look for things you can enjoy doing, even when friends aren't around. This will help you feel happier. It will also give you something to share when you do get together with friends.

Can you think of some things you enjoy doing on your own? Here are some ideas:

* Read an exciting book.

* Practice a sport.

* Watch a movie.

* Cook something delicious.

* Play a game you can do on your own.

* Make a video.

* Play with a pet.

* Build something.

* Make a gift for someone.

* Play or listen to music.

* Rearrange your room or organize your closet.

* Follow your curiosity and learn something new.

Learning to enjoy your own company can help you feel less lonely.

15

The Opposites of Sadness Are Contentment, Gratitude, and Hope

Feeling sad is painful, but it helps us notice when we're missing something. Sadness makes us want to turn inward, but it can also motivate us to seek comfort or make changes.

Feeling sad about friends is about wishing for closeness that's not there. Simon felt sad because his good buddy moved away. Divya felt disappointed because she didn't make it onto the A-team with her friends. Zack's sadness was influenced by shame and envy because he believes he's unlikeable. Kiko's sadness was about feeling lonely because she doesn't have a close friend. The challenge for each of these kids was to notice their feelings and also find ways to move forward, toward the closeness with friends they want.

We talked about lots of ways that these kids could think differently about their situations and also steps they could take to build closeness with friends. Another thing that might help is to focus on feelings that are the opposite of sadness. Even when you're feeling sad, you can have more than that one feeling at the same time. Looking for Opposite Feelings within yourself won't erase sadness, but it can ease the ache.

One feeling that is the opposite of sadness is *contentment*. Feeling *content* means being peaceful and enjoying the small pleasures of the moment.

Feeling Content

Noticing things with your five senses—seeing, hearing, smelling, touching, tasting—can help you find contentment. When you eat dinner, really try to taste your food. Notice the burst of flavor as you bite into it and how that flavor spreads in your mouth. Sit quietly for a moment and notice all the sounds you hear. Do you hear birds tweeting or music playing faintly? When you walk outside, feel the warmth of the sun or the breeze on your face. Notice all the different colors around you. When you wash your hands, smell the scent of the soap and feel the slipperiness of the bubbles.

Obviously, none of these noticings will take away your sadness about friends, but if you pay attention, you can look for these little feelings of contentment *even* when you're feeling sad.

Another feeling that's the opposite of sadness is **gratitude**. Feeling **grateful** means being thankful for the good things in your life.

Gratitude

When you're feeling sad, it can be hard to remember what you're grateful for. Again, feeling grateful won't erase sadness, but it can remind you that there's more going on in your life than sadness. Here are some questions that can help you find grateful feelings within yourself, even when you're sad about friends.

* Who are the people who care about you or help you? You can feel grateful for their presence in your life.

* What do you enjoy doing? You can feel grateful that you're able to do that.

* What topics do you find interesting (either in school or at home)? You can feel grateful that you get to learn about those.

* What makes your life more comfortable? You can feel grateful that you have those things.

* What makes you laugh or smile? You can feel grateful that you've had those experiences.

You may want to take some time each day to write down one thing that you're grateful for. It's easy to notice when something is wrong in your life. It takes practice to be able to notice what's right. Over time, you'll get a big list of the things that you're grateful for. Reading through the list and continuing to add to it builds the habit of seeing more than sadness.

> Hope makes sadness easier to bear.

One other important feeling that's the opposite of sadness is **hope**. We feel **hopeful** when we allow ourselves to believe that things can get better. Hope can help us keep going or inspire us to try something new. It can be hard to find hope when we're feeling sad, but when we can, it makes sadness easier to bear.

169

Hope

When you're feeling sad about friends, notice that—it's important information about what you want or wish for. But try to balance that sadness with feelings of contentment, gratitude, and hope. These involve a soft, gentle kind of happiness. Building close friendships can take awhile, but you can find small pleasures along the way.

THINK ABOUT IT!

Here are some questions to help you think about dealing with sadness about friends:

* Have you ever had a friendship end? What happened? How did you move past that?

* Can you think of a time when you were very disappointed but eventually those feelings faded? Who comforted you then? What did you do to comfort yourself? When did you realize that the feelings weren't as painful anymore?

* Why is it not kind or helpful to put yourself down? Why do you think kids sometimes do that anyway?

* Have you ever felt lonely in a crowd of kids? How did you handle that?

* What have you done, or what could you do, to become closer to your friends?

* What do you find most comforting when you feel sad?

HOW TO COMFORT
A FRIEND

We've talked about lots of ways to deal with your feelings about friends.

But what about your friends' feelings? How can you comfort a buddy who is hurting? When a friend is upset, you may be tempted to try to fix things by leaping in with advice. Often, that's not really what a friend wants. Advice can feel like pressure or a put-down when it comes across as "You should just . . ."

Ugh is right! Jumping in with advice says to a hurting friend, "Your problem is easy!" or "I know better than you do!" That's not at all comforting. So what might be more helpful?

LISTEN FIRST

The first thing to do is just listen to your upset friend and echo their words to show you hear what they're saying. You could say:

* **You**'re feeling _____ because _____ .

* It's hard for **you** when _____ .

* It bothers **you** when _____ .

* **You** wish _____ .

If you're not sure what the friend is feeling, you could add, "It seems like . . ." or "It sounds like . . ." in front of these statements and then listen to what they say in response.

Notice that all of these have the word "you" in them, and they don't have the word "I." That's because, when you're offering comfort, you want the focus to be on your friend, not yourself.

Just echoing your friend's feelings won't solve the problem, but it can help your friend feel like you care and understand. That is comforting. Sometimes friends aren't looking for you to fix things; they just want you to listen.

ASK RATHER THAN TELL

After you've listened, depending on the kind of problem, you may want to ask your friend, "What do you think you're going to do?" This is more respectful than just leaping in and giving advice. It shows you know that your friend is smart and has probably thought about various things they could do.

You might also ask, "What do you think will happen if you do that?" That can help your friend think things through.

If you have an idea that your friend hasn't thought of, you can ask, "I have an idea that might help. Do you want to hear it?" If your friend says no, let it go. It's more important to be comforting to your friend than to be "right."

You could also ask your friend, "What can I do to help?" or "Do you want to talk about this, or would you rather do something else so you don't have to think about it?" The only way to know what your friend wants from you is to ask.

175

DO SOMETHING TO SHOW YOU CARE

If your friend is upset with you, you can show through your actions that you understand what was upsetting them and you're going to do things differently from now on.

No matter what is the cause of your friend's upset, you may want to do an act of kindness for your friend. That might involve spending time with your friend or inviting your friend to do something special with you. Or you might give your upset friend a small gift, such as some cookies you made, something silly that will make your friend laugh, a photo of the two of you, or a note saying how much they mean to you.

Your efforts to comfort your friend may not fix things. Sometimes problems are not easily solved. But showing your friend that you care, especially when they're hurting, can deepen your friendship.

FINAL THOUGHTS: BUILDING STRONG AND HAPPY FRIENDSHIPS

Happiness with friends is a feeling of enjoyment, connection, and comfort. This whole book is about helping you build strong and happy friendships. We've looked at lots and lots of ways you can understand, communicate, and deal with feelings about friends.

We want to leave you with three final tips:

Have fun together. Kids make friends by doing fun things together. Don't let anxious, mad, or sad feelings hold you back from having fun. Enjoying time with friends can lift your mood and bring you and your friends closer.

Work through Friendship Rough Spots. Handling an argument or misunderstanding with a friend in a caring way can help you understand each other better and might even improve your friendship. Be open to hearing and responding to what your friend wants. Explain your feelings clearly and gently, and ask for what you want. (Your friend can't know unless you say!) Sometimes just letting a bit of time pass helps tempers cool. Try not to hold on to old hurts.

Give and receive support from friends. Think about what you can do to show your friends that you care about them. Notice and appreciate when your friends do kind things for you. Let your friends get to know the real you. You're not perfect and neither is your friend. That's OK. True friends treasure each other just as they are.

ACKNOWLEDGMENTS

Relationships are complicated. We wrote this book because we wanted to offer children a nuanced and useful guide for understanding, communicating about, and coping with the feelings that come up around friendships. And we wanted to make kids laugh while learning, so our beloved, butt-sniffing cat and dog characters, whom we introduced in *Growing Friendships*, are here, wandering through the text with their goofy suggestions.

The contents of this book draw as much as possible from research about children's friendships as well as Eileen's work with clients in her private practice as a clinical psychologist in Princeton, New Jersey.

We'd like to thank our dedicated agent, Nicole Geiger of Full Circle Literary, for believing in this book and working enthusiastically to get it out in the world. We'd also like to thank Beyond Words Publishing and our insightful editor, Lindsay Easterbrooks-Brown, for her wise advice on the manuscript, and our illustrator, Cathi Mingus, for thoughtfully bringing our characters to life.

We'd like to thank all the children and parents we've known who have generously spoken with us about their friendship concerns so we could make this book real and relevant. Most of all, we'd like to thank our families: Chris's husband, Bill; and their sons, Joey, Tommy, and Will; and Eileen's husband, Tony; and their children, Mary, Daniel, Sheila, and Brenna. Our families' love, support, and inspiration are invaluable to us.

Eileen Kennedy-Moore, PhD, and Christine McLaughlin

ADDITIONAL RESOURCES FROM DR. KENNEDY-MOORE

FOR KIDS

Growing Friendships: A Kids' Guide to Making and Keeping Friends by Eileen Kennedy-Moore and Christine McLaughlin (Beyond Words/Aladdin, 2017).

Moody Moody Cars by Eileen Kennedy-Moore (Magination Press, 2022).

What About Me? 12 Ways to Get Your Parents' Attention (Without Hitting Your Sister) by Eileen Kennedy-Moore (Parenting Press, 2005).

For funny and useful advice about friendships for kids, check out DrFriendtastic.com and listen to the weekly five-minute podcast for chidren *Kids Ask Dr. Friendtastic* (available on all podcast platforms).

FOR PARENTS

Dr. Friendtastic newsletter for parents with useful tips about children's feelings and friendships: DrFriendtastic.substack.com.

Growing Friendships blog on Psychology Today website: GrowingFriendshipsBlog.com.

Kid Confidence: Help Your Child Make Friends, Build Resilience, and Develop Real Self-Esteem by Eileen Kennedy-Moore (New Harbinger Publications, 2019).

Raising Emotionally and Socially Healthy Kids by Eileen Kennedy-Moore (audio or video series from The Great Courses/Wondrium, 2014). Available for instant download at TheGreatCourses.com /courses/raising-emotionally-and-socially-healthy-kids.html or https://www.wondrium.com/raising-emotionally-and-socially -healthy-kids.

Smart Parenting for Smart Kids: Nurturing Your Child's True Potential by Eileen Kennedy-Moore and Mark S. Lowenthal (Jossey-Bass/ Wiley, 2011).

The Unwritten Rules of Friendship: Simple Strategies to Help Your Child Make Friends by Natalie Madorsky Elman and Eileen Kennedy-Moore (Little, Brown, 2003).

What's My Child Thinking? Practical Child Psychology for Modern Parents by Eileen Kennedy-Moore and Tanith Carey (DK, 2019).

GLOSSARY

acceptance: The feeling and action of liking people the way they are or recognizing that a situation is just how things are right now, rather than expecting them to change. This is an Opposite Feeling to anger.

actions: What you do. Unlike thoughts or feelings, which happen inside you, actions are things that other people could see.

afraid: Feeling anxious about something or someone you think is likely to hurt or upset you in some way.

anger/angry: The feeling that comes when we believe we're being blocked from what we want to do or we're being treated in a way that's unfair. Anger with friends comes up when they do things that we don't like or that we believe are hurtful to us.

anxious/anxiety: The feeling that comes from worrying about *What if something bad happens?* When we feel anxious about friends, it usually involves worrying that other kids won't like us or will think we're dumb, weird, or uncool.

ashamed/shame: Feeling bad because you think you're a bad person or just overall not good enough. Shame is less useful than guilt because it's harder to find a path forward when you believe your whole self (rather than a specific action) is wrong.

Bigger-Than-Me Happiness: The feeling when we choose to do the right thing, especially when it's difficult to do, or when we act in ways that make the world a better place. This is an Opposite Feeling to anger.

brave: Being brave means doing something *even though* you feel scared.

calm: A feeling of being relaxed and comfortable, not at all upset.

common ground: An experience you and another kid share, especially what you both enjoy doing. This is where friendships grow.

compassion: The feeling that comes when we look at someone with kind eyes, not expecting them to be perfect and realizing they have good intentions. We can have compassion for ourselves as well as for others. This is an Opposite Feeling to anger.

compromise: Doing partly what you want and partly what the other person wants.

content/contentment: Feeling peaceful and enjoying the small pleasures of the moment. Contentment is one of the Opposite Feelings of sadness.

context: Seeing an event, such as a mistake, in comparison to everything else. Looking at the full picture of what happened, and why, helps you understand how important or unimportant the event is.

curious/curiosity: The feeling when you wonder and want to discover. This is an Opposite Feeling to anxiety.

disappointed/disappointment: The feeling when we don't get something we want and expected to get.

embarrassed/embarrassment: The feeling of being uncomfortably aware of other people noticing us and worrying that people will judge us negatively.

Emergency First Aid Calming Strategies: Quick strategies to use when you're upset, not to solve a problem, but just to help yourself calm down so you can think. They include slow breathing, doing math facts in your head, and noticing things around you.

Emotional Spillover: When feelings about one situation affect how you respond in a later situation.

emotions: Specific feelings, such as anger, fear, sadness, or jealousy.

Enemy Thinking: Spending a lot of energy watching, judging, and even plotting against someone you strongly dislike.

envy/envious: The feeling when we compare ourselves to others and wish we could be as good as them.

escalate/escalation: When a situation, such as an argument, gets worse and worse.

event: Something that happens. Thoughts and feelings come up in response to an event.

excited/excitement: The feeling when you're eagerly looking forward to something. You might feel all jittery inside, but it's a fun jitteriness. This is an Opposite Feeling to anxiety.

excuse: An argument that tries to explain away some wrong action by saying it's not really wrong.

fear: see *afraid*

feelings: Our inner emotional responses to what's happening in and around us. Feelings can be pleasant or unpleasant, mild or intense. You can have more than one feeling at the same time. What you think and do affects how you feel.

Feelings Families: Groups of similar feelings. Examples include the *anxious*, *angry*, *sad*, or *happy* Feelings Families. It's common to have more than one feeling at the same time, from the same or a different Feelings Family.

Feelings Story: The circle of thoughts, feelings, and actions that we have in response to an event or situation, plus the reactions that our actions bring out from other people. Our thoughts and feelings happen inside us. Our actions and other people's reactions happen outside of us, where other people can see them. Feelings Stories affect how we feel and how strong our relationships are. Changing how we think, feel, or act can move our Feelings Story in a different direction.

flexible: Can bend. People are flexible when they adjust to unexpected events or consider what other people want or need.

Friendship Bag of Marbles: A way of imagining how strong a friendship is. Whenever you and your friend have good times together, it's like you're adding a marble to the bag. Arguing or being mean to a friend rips a hole in the bag and drains the marbles quickly. A full bag means a strong friendship with someone.

Friendship Rough Spot: When friends disagree, upset, or annoy each other. Rough Spots happen in all friendships, but they don't have to mean the end of a relationship.

furious: An intense form of anger. When you're furious, it can feel like you're going to explode with anger. Sometimes people do things they later regret when they're feeling furious.

grateful/gratitude: The feeling of being thankful for the good things in your life. Gratitude is one of the Opposite Feelings of sadness.

Great-Plus-One-Fact Formula: A friendly way to respond to a "How are you?" question. The "great" part expresses enthusiasm. The "one fact" should be something that creates a picture in the listener's mind to help the conversation flow.

grief/grieving: The aching feeling from knowing something or someone you care deeply about is no longer with you.

grumpy: Feeling bothered and a little bit angry about everything

guilt/guilty: The uncomfortable feeling of knowing you've done something wrong. Guilt can help you recognize when you need to make things right or move in a different direction.

happy/happiness: The feeling of enjoyment, connection, and comfort.

hopeful/hope: The feeling of allowing ourselves to believe that things can get better. This is an Opposite Feeling to sadness.

hopeless/hopelessness: The feeling of sadness when we do not think that the future will be better.

hurt: Hurt can be an action, when we do something that causes someone pain, either in their body or their feelings. Hurt can also be a feeling, when we feel sad or upset because of something someone did that makes it seem like they don't care about us.

intention: What someone is trying to do. A good intention means trying to be kind. A bad intention means trying to be mean. A neutral intention is neither—it might have nothing to do with you.

irritated: A low-level angry feeling when someone or something just bothers us.

jealous/jealousy: The feeling of fear and protectiveness that comes up when we believe another person might hurt or even break up our close friendship.

Keeping-Score Mindset: The perspective that you always need to be on the lookout for anything that might be unfair to you.

lonely/loneliness: Feeling painfully disconnected from people. This can happen even when others are nearby.

mad: A kind of angry feeling that is directed at a certain person or thing. You can be mad at a friend.

making amends: After you've done something wrong, the action to do what you can to make the situation right, either now or in the future.

mean: Unkind actions. Also, the feeling of wanting to upset or hurt someone. May involve wanting to get even with someone who has hurt you.

nervous: Feeling anxious and jumpy inside because of what you imagine could go wrong.

Opposite Feelings: Feelings that move us in a different direction. They can balance out and sometimes replace painful feelings. They are aspects of happiness.

186

playful/playfulness: Feeling silly and lighthearted. This is an Opposite Feeling to anxiety.

preference: When you notice that you'd rather have one situation instead of another, but you know you can deal with whatever happens.

reactions: How other people respond to what you do.

reassurance: When you're looking for reassurance, you want someone else to say something that magically makes your worries disappear. This usually makes anxiety worse because no matter how many times someone says, "Don't worry! Nothing bad will happen!" you can always come up with another "But what if . . . ?"

rigid: Can't bend. People can sometimes be rigid in their thoughts and actions when they insist that something has to be a certain way.

sad/sadness: The feeling of unhappiness when we're missing something or someone. Sadness helps us figure out what matters to us. It can lead us to seek comfort, which brings us closer to others. It can also inspire us to make changes to try to fill in what's missing.

scared/scary: The anxious feeling we get when something seems dangerous or overwhelming, because we don't know how to handle it.

See the Bigger Picture: Looking beyond what you want by considering what others think, feel, want, or need.

self-conscious: The feeling of being uncomfortably aware of everything you might be doing wrong or everything about you that's not perfect, especially when you think other people are watching and judging you.

shame: see *ashamed*.

shy: Feeling uncomfortable around people you don't know well because you're not sure what to say or do, and you're worried they won't like you.

Social Detective: You are a Social Detective when you watch carefully to figure out what other kids are doing in a certain situation.

taking responsibility for our actions: Admitting what we did wrong and doing what we can to make things better going forward.

thoughts: Your ideas about what something means or what might happen. Thoughts are not the same as facts. Facts can be checked and everyone can agree on them, but people can have different thoughts about the meaning of certain facts or events. Thoughts can lead to feelings.

Tiny-Bit-Empty Thinking: Getting stuck focusing on the tiniest thing that is not exactly how you want. This kind of thinking makes people very unhappy.

vulnerable/vulnerability: The feeling when you let someone know you well enough that you could get hurt. That's a risk, but if you choose wisely, being willing to be vulnerable makes it possible to have a close friendship.

Well-at-Least Game: A strategy that involves imagining a worse situation than the one you're facing so the actual disappointment doesn't seem so bad.

worried: Feeling anxious because we keep thinking about possible problems and how difficult they would be.

wronged: Feeling angry because something seems unfair.

ABOUT THE AUTHORS

Eileen Kennedy-Moore, PhD, is an author, psychologist, and mom of four. She is a trusted expert on parenting and child development who is frequently featured in major media, such as the *New York Times*, the *Washington Post*, and *Live with Kelly and Ryan*. Her most recent books for children are *Moody Moody Cars* and *Growing Friendships: A Kids' Guide to Making and Keeping Friends* (written with Christine McLaughlin). She has also written four books for parents. Her books have been translated into ten languages. Dr. Kennedy-Moore is the creator of the *Kids Ask Dr. Friendtastic* podcast, which features friendship advice for kids. Her blog, *Growing Friendships*, on Psychology Today, has over 4.9 million views. Dr. Kennedy-Moore has a private practice in Princeton, New Jersey (lic. #35SI00425400), where she works with adults, children, and families.

Check out EileenKennedyMoore.com.

Christine McLaughlin is a mom to three boys, as well as a prolific writer, editor, and author. With several hundred nonfiction articles to her credit—published in popular magazines and websites—her written work focuses mainly on parenting and health topics. She is the author of eight books including *Growing Friendships: A Kids' Guide to Making and Keeping Friends* (written with Dr. Eileen Kennedy-Moore), *The Dog Lover's Companion to Philadelphia*, and *American Red Cross: Dog First Aid* and *American Red Cross: Cat First Aid*. She and her family live in the Philadelphia area.

Check out ChristineMcLaughlin.net.

GROWING FRIENDSHIPS

A KIDS' GUIDE TO
Making and Keeping Friends

By Dr. Eileen Kennedy-Moore
& Christine McLaughlin

A FUNNY AND USEFUL GUIDE TO HELP CHILDREN NAVIGATE THEIR SOCIAL WORLD. FILLED WITH CARTOONS AND RESEARCH-BASED TIPS.

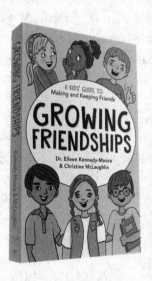

Part 1: Reaching Out to Make Friends

Part 2: Stepping Back to Keep Friends

Part 3: Blending In to Join Friends

Part 4: Speaking Up to Share with Friends

Part 5: Letting Go to Accept Friends

"The secret playbook you'll wish you'd had when you were growing up."

Diane Debrovner, executive editor, *Parents* magazine